Advanced Praise for
The Seven Strategies of Master Negotiators

An insightful book that distils the lessons of success across different walks of life. If you want to know what is needed to win, read this carefully.

— **Michael Sabia**
President, Bell Canada Enterprises

Many books tell you how to negotiate, but Brad McRae walks you through the steps with real-life examples taken directly from interviews with some of Canada's best negotiators. You must read this book before your next negotiation!

— **Steven J. Stein**
CEO of Multi-Health Systems and
Co-author of *The EQ Edge*

We are all required to negotiate on behalf of ourselves, our families, or the organization we represent. Brad McRae has created an informative guide to improving this essential skill. A valuable read!

— **David Rathbun**
Chief Human Resources Officer, Aliant Inc.

Negotiations are part of everyone's life; therefore, one has to be as well prepared as possible in order to take pleasure in them. This book is enjoyable reading and can be helpful for that purpose.

— **Paul Tellier**
CEO, Canadian National Railroad

Not just another book on negotiation ... new perspectives, insights and strategies from some of Canada's best will help you plan for and build successful solutions and winning agreements.

— **Linda Tarrant**
Certified Speaking Professional

The Seven Strategies are clear and easy to understand. The stories ... are engaging and shed light on how the strategies are implemented in real life.

— **Bob Gardiner**
E-Business Guide

The SEVEN STRATEGIES *of* MASTER NEGOTIATORS

Dr. Brad McRae

McGraw-Hill
Ryerson

Toronto Montréal Boston Burr Ridge, IL Dubuque, IA Madison, WI New York
San Francisco St. Louis Bangkok Bogotá Caracas Kuala Lumpur Lisbon London
Madrid Mexico City Milan New Delhi Santiago Seoul Singapore Sydney Taipei

McGraw-Hill
Ryerson Limited
    *A Subsidiary of The **McGraw-Hill** Companies*

ISBN: 007-089887-1

1234567890 WEB 098765432

National Library of Canada Cataloguing in Publication Data

McRae, Bradley C. (Bradley Collins), 1945–

   The seven strategies of master negotiators

Includes bibliographical references and index.

ISBN 0-07-089887-1

1. Negotiation. 2. Negotiation in business. I. Title.

HD58.6.M38   2002   658.4'052   C2001-903893-3

Publisher: Joan Homewood

Editorial Co-ordinator: Catherine Leek

Production Co-ordinator: Sandra Deak

Editor: Katherine Coy of Wordworks

Electronic Page Design and Composition: Heidy Lawrance Associates

Cover Design: Silver Birch Graphics/Monica Koupter

Cover Image: © Bill Frymire/Masterfile

Printed and bound in Canada.

This book is dedicated to the teachers and mentors with whose help and guidance I started on the road to life-long learning: my late father, Collins McRae, who encouraged my curiosity and keen desire to find out how things work; Henry Peterson, former professor of psychology at California State University at Chico who inspired me to teach by the example he set; Ken Boyce, former vice-president of sales at the Atlantic Television System, who encouraged me to start my own business, and lastly to my two wonderful children Andrew Collins McRae and Kathryn Crosby McRae who delight in providing additional lessons on the road to life-long learning.

Lastly, a portion of the profits from this book will be dedicated to Pier 21 to continue the wonderful work that they are doing to honour Canada's past so we can more effectively build the future.

Table of Contents

Preface

I have written *The Seven Strategies of Master Negotiators* because these skills are the foundation on which we need to build our futures, both personal and professional. As you read this book and develop the Seven Strategies used by Master Negotiators, you, like the thousands of participants I have taught in my seminars and keynotes, will find that your life becomes both challenging and more rewarding.

Skill development in negotiating and influencing skills is much like parenting. Our parenting skills have to change and adapt as we and our children grow older. The skills that work perfectly well with a six-year-old will not work at all with a 16-year-old. Turning to the workplace, as work becomes more and more complex, and as our work requires an ever increasing amount of cooperation and teamwork, developing, enhancing and refining our skills in negotiating and influencing have never been more important. In your journey to learn the Seven Strategies, I wish you God's speed.

There are many people I would like to thank for their help and support in the writing of this book. My sincere thanks to all of the Master Negotiators I interviewed for this book: Lloyd Axworthy, former foreign affairs minister; Bill Black, president and CEO of Maritime Life; Stella Campbell, former chairperson of the Halifax Regional School Board; Bernd Christmas, CEO

Membertou Band; Eric Claus, general manager and CEO of CO-OP Atlantic; Janet Conners, AIDS activist; Frank King, XVth Winter Olympics; Neville Gilfoy, publisher of *Atlantic Progress* magazine; Ruth Goldbloom, Order of Canada recipient for Pier 21; Kevin Hamm, president and CEO of Pharmasave Atlantic; Buzz Hargrove, president of the Canadian Auto Workers Union; Major-General (Ret'd) Lewis MacKenzie; Frank McKenna, former premier of New Brunswick; David Mowat, president and CEO of Vancouver City Saving Credit Union; David Rathbun, chief human resources officer of Aliant, Inc.; Dawna Ring, lawyer, legal council to the Krever Commission; Isadore Sharp, chairman and CEO of Four Seasons Hotel Inc.; Dr. Nicholas Steinmetz, associate executive director for planning of the McGill University Health Centre; Harold Taylor, president and CEO of Harold Taylor Time Consultants Inc.; Paul Tellier, president and CEO of the Canadian National Railroad; and Annette Verschuren, president of Home Depot Canada. Each of these Master Negotiators added significantly to my understanding of the Seven Strategies of Master Negotiators.

I would also like to acknowledge the following people, without whose help and support this book could not have been written: Glenn Sutherland, whose job it was to keep my computers and software working, Mary-Beth Clark and Lawrence McEachern, my home editing team, and my editors, Joan Homewood and Catherine Leek at McGraw-Hill Ryerson, and Katherine Coy of Wordworks. If I were ever to write a book on Master Editors, Joan would be the first person I would write about. Lastly I would like to thank my support team, my two wonderful children, Andrew and Kathryn McRae, and my two best friends, John Loback and Terrye Perlman.

Brad McRae
Halifax, N.S.
January, 2002

Introduction: Setting the Stage

For the past 16 years, I have been teaching thousands of people from all walks of life to negotiate more effectively. During that time, I have emphasized repeatedly that negotiation is made up of a symphony of strategies and skills, and each skill and strategy directly contributes to the overall success of the negotiation. During the research and writing of this book and through interviewing Master Negotiators, I have found that this expression is even more valid than I had originally thought. Over and over again, I have seen Master Negotiators use the right strategy and the right tool, in the right way, and at the right time. The Master Negotiators that I studied also had the flexibility to change the strategies and skills that they used in relation to the fluidity of the negotiation process. It does not matter if you are negotiating a merger on behalf of a major organization, fundraising, advocating for social justice or talking to your teenage son or daughter about how loud he or she plays their music. We all negotiate and we negotiate all of the time.

Organization of *The Seven Strategies of Master Negotiators*

The purpose of this book is to help the reader develop the skills and strategies used by the Master Negotiators I studied. The Seven Strategies are:

1. Build the Future with Creative Solutions
2. Come to the Table Incredibly Well-Prepared
3. Create and Claim Maximum Value
4. Understand Negotiating Styles
5. Manage the Negotiation Process
6. Build Strategic Alliances
7. Become a Life-Long Learner

All totaled, I conducted interviews with 21 Canadian Master Negotiators. There were four criteria that I used in selecting the Master Negotiators to be interviewed:

1. they had to make Canada or the world a better place;
2. they had to have predominately used their negotiating and influencing skills to have done so;
3. they had to have a proven track record; and
4. the types of people interviewed had to be from as diverse backgrounds as possible.

Although the Master Negotiators I interviewed all had distinct personalities, one thing they had in common was their expert use of the Seven Strategies. Short biographies on each of the 21 Master Negotiators I interviewed appear in The Who's Who of Master Negotiators at the back of this book.

The Seven Strategies of Master Negotiators were derived from my experience teaching negotiating and influencing skills, from interviewing Master Negotiators, and from an extensive review of books and articles on negotiating and influencing skills. Each of the Seven Strategies is summarized at the end of this chapter and is explored in depth in subsequent sections of this book. In fact, the strategy numbering is reflected in the organization of the book, with each chapter representing a strategy. Each chapter also contains one or more challenging examples that demonstrate how each of the Seven Strategies can be applied. These examples invite you to watch some of the world's best negotiators as they develop creative solutions to interesting and challenging problems.

The examples, interviews and exercises cover a wide range of challenges from business, to peacekeeping, to community development. The ultimate goal of this book is for you to learn the skills and strategies necessary to develop more creative solutions to the problems you encounter both in your personal and professional life. Detailed exercises are included throughout the book. Completing the exercises and practising the skills will help you transfer your good intentions into action.

To introduce you to how the strategies are used, we will now turn to three interviews with Master Negotiators, one from the volunteer sector, one from the private sector and one from government. These are three very different people, from very different settings, but what they have in common is their incredible levels of accomplishment. The interviews will be used to introduce and illustrate some of the strategies used by Master Negotiators.

Ruth Goldbloom and Pier 21

Pier 21 National Historic Site is a tribute to the immigrants who have passed through its doors and helped Canada develop into a diverse and strong nation. Between 1928 and 1971, over one million immigrants and 58,000 war brides entered Canada and close to half a million military personnel who served overseas during World War II passed through Pier 21 in Halifax, Nova Scotia. Pier 21 National Historic Site was named the Best New Attraction in Canada in 2001.

Ruth Goldbloom is the driving force behind the establishment of the Pier 21 National Historic Site. She is a grandmother of seven, a philanthropist, fundraiser, speaker extraordinaire and a role model for us all. Ruth was the president of the Pier 21 Historical Society from 1993 to 1999. During those six years she went to work at 7:30 every morning and came home between 5 and 7 every night. During her tenure, the Pier 21 Historical Society raised over $9 million for the Pier 21 project. For her accomplishments she was awarded the Order of Canada in April, 2000.

By the time my interview with Ruth was over, I could see clearly why this woman was one of the most successful fundraisers in Canadian history. Like all Master Negotiators, she has a keen vision of precisely what needs to be done, and her vision is fuelled by her passion and enthusiasm. This charismatic leader has the ability to make people want to contribute and to bring out the greater good that is in us all.

B.M. *What is your vision for Pier 21?*

R.G. When I was invited to join the Pier 21 Society—this entryway—this gateway to Canada was a derelict, pigeon- and rat-infested building on the Halifax waterfront. Our vision was to turn it into a compellingly interactive tribute to the over one million people who immigrated to Canada and passed through its doors from 1928 to 1971. We wanted to turn it into something that would tell future generations about the people, who in passing through its doors, had made such a tremendous impact on this country.

Pier 21 is Canada's Ellis Island. I have been to Ellis Island twice, and what we have done is so much more interactive: for example, we have a multimedia exhibit called "Oceans of Hope" and a "train" that [you] can take across Canada and discover what it was like to be an immigrant to this vast country. In fact, one in five Canadian families can claim an association with Pier 21.

The heartbeat of what we have done is to make the exhibition hall one of the most compelling and interactive historical sites in the world. *Le Devoir* has said that the only thing missing from Pier 21 is a large box of Kleenex. We had no idea we would touch a nerve across the country like we have and that Pier 21 would be declared a national historic site.

I did not get the sense that this dynamic woman was about to retire, but before I could ask her what her next project was, she enthusiastically told me that even though Pier 21 was up and running and was a phenomenal success, there were still a lot more things that needed to be done. For example, "We need funds so every school child of an appropriate age from across Atlantic Canada can spend a day at the site and see how our past has affected our present. We must also raise money to continue researching and videotaping the people who have gone though Pier 21. If we don't capture their stories now, they are gone forever."

Although Ruth is now past president of the Pier 21 Historical Society, she has become the principal spokesperson for Pier 21 and is a much sought-after speaker. Not only does she have a vision of what she wants to accomplish, but also she has learned to bring her message to her audience in a meaningful way.

B.M. *How do you approach your audiences when speaking about Pier 21?*

R.G. You know, for a country of immigrants, we often perceive the word "immigrant" negatively so I always ask my audience, "How many in the room are immigrants?" Usually one or two hands go up. When I ask, "How many of your parents were immigrants?" usually eight to 10 hands go up. When I ask, "How many of your grandparents were immigrants?" 40 to 60 percent of the hands in the room go up.

I then startle my audience by saying that, "If today's immigration rules applied in 1909, I wouldn't be here today because under the current immigration laws, my family would not have qualified.

Ruth Goldbloom is, not surprisingly, a master at developing strategic alliances, one of the Seven Strategies demonstrated by many Master Negotiators. She knows foundations from coast to coast, and of course they know Ruth. She has received much support from all kinds of people: "I had a wonderful local and national advisory board [at Pier 21]; they wrote letters on their personal stationery and persuaded other powerful people they knew to join this worthy cause."

B.M.   *Could you give me an example of an alliance that worked for you in Pier 21?*

R.G.   I made one phone call to the late Peter Bronfman. I said we needed his help and I had breakfast with him. Peter Bronfman said he wasn't particularly good at fundraising but he would introduce me to Senator Trevor Eyton. Peter sent my information over to Senator Eyton and we met a few minutes later. Trevor read the material and said he couldn't help because he was so busy on the boards of six companies and was involved in several other fundraising causes.

I didn't say anything, but just looked at him and waited. Senator Eyton then said that his fall back position was that he would do it if Peter did it with him.

Ruth got two for one. Ruth also asked Martin Connell, who headed up the "Imagine Program" to join the Pier 21 Advisory Board. She said, "The Imagine Program asks that every corporation in Canada give 1 percent of their pre-tax dollars to the charity of their choice. He [Martin Connell] came on board and that made a tremendous difference. It's like dropping a rock in a pond; it makes ripples."

Each and every Master Negotiator I interviewed had both the passion and the commitment to move mountains in order to bring their dreams to fruition. I asked Ruth about her strong commitment to the Pier 21 National Historical Site. She simply said, "Each time I heard another story, I knew that what I was doing was right. We make a living by what we get, we make a life from what we give—the rewards were all mine." Ruth's ultimate goal was to leave the country with something that it didn't have before. In that goal, she has succeeded admirably.

> *Paul Tellier has an incredibly strong vision, he was able to develop strategic alliances and he had the dedication, creative problem solving and negotiating skills to make it work.*

Paul Tellier and the Canadian National Railroad

When **Paul Tellier** became the president and CEO of the Canadian National Railroad in October, 1992, he had two major strikes against him. Firstly, he had never worked in the railroad industry. Secondly, the organization for which he was at the helm was known as "a state-owned monster, and a heavily bureaucratic and money losing one at that." So how did Paul turn CN into one of the most effective and efficient railroads in North America? Like Ruth Goldbloom, Paul Tellier has an incredibly strong vision, he was able to develop strategic alliances and he had the dedication, creative problem solving and negotiating skills to make it work.

Significantly, as I began the interview with Paul, he told me that he had prepared by reading all of the background material that I had sent him, including the sample questions that I wanted to ask, and by making notes on the Sunday evening before the interview took place. In other words, he was well-prepared. The fact that Paul prepared for the interview tells us a great deal about the importance that Master Negotiators place on preparation. As the interview proceeded, I also learned that Paul, like all Master Teachers, always uses precise examples to illustrate his points. I also noticed how he put me at ease right from the start of our conversation. Although I had never spoken to him before, his focused, yet easygoing manner was like talking to a favourite neighbour across the back fence—only this favourite neighbour runs a $5.4 billion a year company.

Paul Tellier's negotiating style is to be incredibly well-prepared, informative, insightful and personable as the following interview demonstrates.

B.M.   *Can you describe your negotiating style?*

P.T.   I believe in establishing a good rapport with the people across the table in order to know what kind of a person or persons they are. It is important to get to know their interests, if they have children or grandchildren, if they like sports, or their philosophy of work.

Secondly, and this is a point that cannot be overstated: You have to be prepared every which way about the people, the subject and your fallback position. I want to be sure that we will not be blindsided. Sometimes my colleagues think that I over prepare, but usually I have a dry run. Before walking into the room for the actual negotiation, I ask my colleagues to throw some curve balls at me. So in addition to developing rapport, it is essential to be thoroughly well-prepared.

Thirdly, I always try to put myself in the other party's shoes. You have to realize what you are asking them to accept from their point of view. For example, when we entered into the transaction to merge the Burlington Northern and Santa Fe Railroad and Canadian National, we had an important meeting with their board at their headquarters in Fort Worth, Texas. The issue we were talking about was establishing the headquarters for the combined railroad in Montreal [Quebec]. Now Montreal is a long way from Texas, and my accent is considerably different from theirs. So I had to put myself in their shoes. The Americans in general, and in the Southwest in particular, are very U.S.-centric.

B.M. *Saying that the southwestern United States is very ethnocentric is probably a huge understatement. How did you approach them on such an incredibly sensitive issue?*

P.T. I did it by saying to these people things such as we are not going to run this from Montreal, that the combined railroad would be a decentralized operation. I said that, "If it's not broken, we are not going to fix it," and that most of them would remain working right in the same building where they were currently working. I also suggested that the location of the head office is a legal term and that the head office could have six people in it or 6,000. In addition, I emphasized that the executive offices would be based in Chicago, which is about half-way between Fort Worth and Montreal. They soon started to become more comfortable with the idea.

The next point is to develop a win/win situation for all parties. For instance, when we bought Illinois Central Railroad, I asked their president to be CN's COO [Chief Operating Officer] and I invited their chairman to join our board. When we shook hands, there were no hard feelings. Both sides felt that they got a good deal for their shareholders. Today when we joke, I tell him that we still paid too much.

The last point I wrote down in preparing for this conversation is that you need a firm bottom line while showing the greatest possible flexibility. For example, we just bought Illinois Central Railroad. I often said that the price we would pay would start with a 3. That is we would pay $30 something, but not $40 per share. I never use the phrase; "I am drawing a line in the sand." We ended up paying $39. When we bought Wisconsin Central, I added another 15¢ per share to the offer, and that 15¢ meant a lot to them. It's important to show some flexibility and try to arrive at a *quid pro quo* and give the other guy what he wants without sacrificing our bottom line. In other words, one of my guiding principles as a negotiator is that it is better to leave the last quarter on the table and never ever underestimate the importance of goodwill.

B.M.   *What is your vision of CN in particular and your vision for railroad transportation in the future?*

P.T.   Our vision is to become the best transportation company in North America. No matter what ratio, operating ratio or whatever way you look at, we are a country mile ahead of every one else and have done so for the past 12 consecutive quarters. And that's not good enough. We want to be in the top niche all by ourselves. To use a sport analogy, the Chicago Bulls, thanks to Michael Jordan and others, were in a class all by themselves. To become a dynasty like that, they had to play the game at a different level than all the others. We want to be the Chicago Bulls of the North American railroad industry.

B.M.   *What is your vision for the railroad industry for Canada?*

P.T.   I wouldn't say for Canada alone because there has been a tremendous consolidation. There are now six of us, four in the U.S., with two east of the Mississippi and two west of the Mississippi, and two in Canada. Eventually in the years ahead we will move to either two networks or two companies. Therefore, what is important to Canadians is to ensure that we are the backbone of the transportation industry in both countries. Consequently, it is essential that Canadian shippers have access to a highly competitive transportation mode; that's why we want to provide them with a low cost structure, low rates and efficient service. So no matter if you are shipping coal, wheat, forest products or cars, it is important that [you] can rely on an efficient railroad.

B.M. *What is your approach to life-long learning?*

P.T. I am fascinated by the subject of leadership. I am always reading books on leadership. I have been going to [the] Davos, Switzerland Economic Forum for a number of years and my prime focus is on leadership. I also try to meet and talk with as many leaders as I can. For example, I am a great fan of Jack Welch[1] and have been able to get to know him personally. We have also instituted a strong leadership program at CN, where we look at what leaders do, how they provide leadership and how we review our leadership. For me, learning is the most interesting thing in life.

The interview with Paul Tellier clearly shows the emphasis that he places on coming to the negotiating table impeccably well-prepared and his use of creative problem solving to develop optimal solutions. One of the remarkable things I noticed, in addition to the fact that all Master Negotiators use the Seven Strategies, is the vision and passion they bring to everything they do. For example, if Ruth Goldbloom's vision was to bring Pier 21 to fruition, and Paul Tellier's vision is for CN to be the Chicago Bulls of the North American Railroads, then Frank McKenna's vision was to transform a province.

Frank McKenna and the Province of New Brunswick

Frank McKenna was the premier of New Brunswick from 1987 to 1997. During that time, he worked tirelessly on changing the image New Brunswickers had of themselves and of their province. Before Frank, New

Brunswick was viewed as a backward, have-not province, dependent on its natural resources, the Irving empire and transfer payments. In his time as premier, Frank would work to develop a vision of a "self-sufficient province powered by a state-of-the-art telecommunications industry that would capitalize on New Brunswick's bilingual workforce."[2] His vision was backed by negotiation after negotiation—no matter how big or how small—with businesses in Canada and around the world to bring jobs to New Brunswick.

One result of his efforts was that New Brunswick became the call centre capital of Canada. By the summer of 1999, over 8,000 jobs had been created in New Brunswick in over 55 call centres. However, few people know the full extent of Frank McKenna's commitment to creating jobs in his home province. The following story demonstrates this commitment to creative solutions.

Campobello Island, New Brunswick is located off the coast of Maine. It is most famous for being the summer residence of Franklin Delano Roosevelt. The island is linked to Maine by a 100-metre bridge. The residents of Campobello Island wanted to have a grocery store on their island but there were two major obstacles. Firstly, there were not enough residents on the island to support a store, and secondly, there were not enough funds among the stakeholders to pay for the construction of a store.

CO-OP Atlantic was interested in establishing a CO-OP store on the island. Since there were not enough residents on the island to support a store, the only option was to sign up enough prospective customers across the bridge on the American side. Two hundred American families signed on along with the 300 families from Campobello Island who signed up; that was a large enough population base to support a store. However, the negotiations had reached an impasse on funding for construction of the store. On the last day of the negotiations, Premier McKenna dropped in to see if he could help to further the negotiations. He pushed for the jobs and the sale of New Brunswick products, for concessions from all of the stakeholders, and secured grant monies from the provincial and federal governments. As a result, a store, a pharmacy and a small restaurant were built on the island and 10 additional jobs were created in New Brunswick.

This is an excellent example of a win/win/win negotiation. CO-OP Atlantic was able to establish another store and revenue stream; the province of New Brunswick was able to create 10 additional jobs and has now recouped its investment grants in taxes; and the residents of Campobello Island and the American residents who live across the bridge have ready access to a grocery story, a pharmacy and an Italian restaurant. All of this would not have happened without Frank McKenna's vision, determination and commitment, backed up by his use of superb negotiating and influencing skills, to arrive at optimal rather than sub-optimal solutions.

B.M. *What was your vision as premier of New Brunswick?*

F.M. Jobs, jobs and more jobs! Jobs were at the forefront of all of our strategies—to restore peoples' sense of pride and dignity—to realize that we could compete with the best of the world and win. My emphasis was to increase the number of jobs to help give the citizens of New Brunswick a sense of pride. And the jobs and sense of pride would create a self-fulfilling prophecy.

B.M. *How did you communicate this vision?*

F.M. The key to communication is to highlight two or three important messages, or people will be confused with what you stand for. We focused on jobs. This was important to every decision we made because they affect revenue, taxes, health care and education. I talked about it incessantly. I tried to draw the message out so people could see how all the dots were connected. We wanted to create a self-sufficient province—all of the good things will come from that.

Like Paul Tellier, Frank McKenna appreciates the value of preparation in negotiating. Not only is he well-briefed going in but also he is sensitive to the value-creation aspect of every negotiation. Master Negotiators clearly understand the essence of creating and claiming optimal value, and knowing the parties with whom they negotiate.

B.M. *Can you tell me more about knowing the parties with whom you negotiate?*

F.M. I find that getting to know the other [parties] and getting to understand their needs and interests are critical to a successful negotiation. Fortunately, in government, we had excellent civil servants who prepared excellent briefings; we had to know the person we were dealing with and what made them tick. We had to know what was a "win" for the other party because if you don't know what that is, you can't meet it. For example, in negotiating to get the call centres to come to our province, we had to know about their interests as far as location, turnover and the quality of the workforce and how they prioritized each of these interests.

As with all of the people I interviewed, I asked Frank about the importance of self-control in the negotiation process. His response was, "[I]n a number of areas I had self-control and in a number of areas I did not."

B.M. *Tell me more about self-control and negotiations.*

F.M. In a number of situations, such as union negotiations, I quickly learned that my impatience was a disadvantage to bargaining and it intruded into the process and cost us more money. I learned to reserve the Office of the Premier only for final resolutions when that became necessary. In negotiating with businesses I wanted to get to the end of the deal very quickly, and thus had a tendency to give too much away. Therefore, I left the financial details until the end of the negotiation. I used my strengths where they could work to achieve a common sense of results at the highest level and then let others negotiate the details.

As with all good leaders and managers, we must know our strengths and our weaknesses and in turn capitalize on our strengths, and then either correct our weaknesses or develop a team approach where other team members have those particular talents that we are lacking. Developing a clear understanding of your own negotiating style is as important as understanding the style of those with whom you are negotiating.

> *I used my strengths where they could work to achieve a common sense of results at the highest level and then let others negotiate the details.*
>
> **Frank McKenna**

B.M. *What importance do you place on strategic alliances in the negotiating process?*

F.M. Strategic alliances are critical to success—you absolutely need champions to work with you—to travel with you to get to the desired results. In New Brunswick, our strategic alliance with NBTel was the cornerstone to every success we had.

The Seven Strategies of Master Negotiators

How did Ruth, Paul, Frank and the other Master Negotiators I interviewed accomplish as much as they did, often against seemingly impossible odds? Whether it is Ruth Goldbloom's ability to fundraise, Paul Tellier's ability to build a world-class railroad or Frank McKenna's ability to help transform a province, the answer is through the judicious use of the Seven Strategies. The purpose of this book, therefore, is to help you better understand and develop the Seven Strategies so that you can accomplish more easily and quickly your most important personal and professional goals. Below is a short description of each of the Seven Strategies.

STRATEGY 1: BUILD THE FUTURE WITH CREATIVE SOLUTIONS

Einstein said, "You can't solve a problem with the same kind of thinking that created it." It is that same type of innovative thinking that is at the heart of all successful negotiations.

Strategy 1 examines the power of creating optimal, rather than sub-optimal solutions. Six steps are examined that are guaranteed to increase your ability to think outside the box and to more fully access benefits from others' creative ideas. Interesting examples of outside-the-box thinking will be presented in this Strategy as well as through the rest of the book.

STRATEGY 2: COME TO THE TABLE INCREDIBLY WELL-PREPARED

Master Negotiators always come to the table incredibly well-prepared, while amateur negotiators come to the table overly confident and under prepared. You will also find out that Master Negotiators always have a "plan B," and balance preparedness with flexibility. Master Negotiators always expect the unexpected, no matter how well-prepared they are, and are flexible enough to turn potential problems into opportunities.

STRATEGY 3: CREATE AND CLAIM MAXIMUM VALUE

Creating value is our ability to develop solutions to best meet the needs and interests of all of the parties at the negotiating table. Claiming value is our ability to get our needs and interests met through the negotiating process. Strategy 3 contains an important exercise that assists you in measuring how well you create and claim value. Building on this exercise, seven steps are presented to help you in developing and enhancing these critical skills.

STRATEGY 4: UNDERSTAND NEGOTIATING STYLES

Master Negotiators have developed a clear understanding of their own negotiating style and where it works for them versus where it works against them.
They have also developed a clear understanding of their partners' styles and
have learned how to negotiate effectively with various styles. Lastly, Master
Negotiators know the importance of developing incredible self-control, so
that they control their shadow style rather than their shadow style controlling them.

STRATEGY 5: MANAGE THE NEGOTIATION PROCESS

Master Negotiators have to wear trifocals; that is, they have learned to keep
one eye on the substantive outcome, one eye on relationships and one eye on
the process. If any of these three focuses are lost or not given enough attention, we run the risk of not negotiating as well as we should or could.

Among the skills that will be explored in Strategy 5 are 12 techniques for
improving the negotiation process. In addition, examples are provided that
demonstrate how each of these skills and techniques are used to enhance
negotiating ability.

STRATEGY 6: BUILD STRATEGIC ALLIANCES

Although it often looks like events are accomplished by dint of individual
effort, if we look underneath most major accomplishments, we will see that
much of what was accomplished is the result of building strategic alliances.
Master Negotiators understand this principle and have become experts at
building strategic alliances.

STRATEGY 7: BECOME A LIFE-LONG LEARNER

Strategy 7 covers five critical areas necessary to become a life-long learner,
three of which are: obtaining salient feedback; learning from coaches, mentors and mastermind groups; and learning how to think like the experts.
Learning can also occur through interviewing the best negotiators and

influencers you can find and through accessing the best books, movies and training courses. The Resources from the Masters: An Annotated Bibliography—located at the end of the book—will help accelerate your learning from books, articles and movies and the list of selected courses and training institutions can help maximize learning. Strategy 7 also includes exercises to help you fully develop the strategy of becoming a dedicated life-long learner.

In addition to learning the Seven Strategies used by all Master Negotiators, selected skills and techniques used by Master Negotiators will be examined. Negotiating is a symphony of skills. The reader will learn which of these skills he or she has mastered and which need improvement. Specifically designed exercises are included to help you to develop or enhance each of the strategies. This book also presents real life examples, which demonstrate how those skills and strategies have been used effectively by Master Negotiators.

---

[1] A former president of General Electric, and considered by many to be the most effective CEO of our time.

[2] Philip Lee. *Frank: The Life and Politics of Frank McKenna*. Fredericton, N.B.: Goose Lane Editions, 2001.

STRATEGY 1

Build the Future
with Creative Solutions

You cannot solve a problem with the same kind of thinking that created it.

— *Albert Einstein*

M aster Negotiators build their future with optimum rather than sub-optimal solutions. Finding creative solutions is important to the negotiation process because unless the parties can get their needs and interests reasonably well satisfied, the negotiations often become derailed. As well, many problems that appear to be unsolvable are solvable, if we use creative, innovative, outside-the-box thinking. For all of these reasons, Master Negotiators must learn how to think as creatively as possible

In Strategy 1, we will explore six steps to increase your ability to think outside the box and how to more fully access and benefit from the creative ideas of others. This chapter provides examples of how vision can be turned into a compelling advantage and ends with practical exercises to help you develop and enhance your ability to build your world with creative solutions.

Seven Examples of Creative Solutions

The best way to help you understand what I mean by creative solutions is to present seven pertinent examples:

1. The Mexico City Airport negotiation;
2. Increased safety at no cost;
3. Canadian National Railroad's Sarnia-Port Huron tunnel;
4. Saskatchewan's Habitat for Humanity;
5. The San Francisco Airport car rental shuttle bus program;
6. Radical change in a First Nations band; and
7. Innovative changes bring forth a new kind of financial institution.

Numerous other examples will be presented throughout the book.

THE MEXICO CITY AIRPORT NEGOTIATION

In the early 1970s the mayor of Mexico City wanted to build a new airport. After all, Mexico City was the capital of Mexico and such an important city should have a new, state-of-the-art, airport. So the mayor commissioned studies that proved that Mexico City needed a modern up-to-date airport. At the same time, the Department of Communications and Transportation for the Mexican federal government was seriously concerned about the high levels of pollution in Mexico City. So the Department of Communications and Transportation hired their own experts who proved that building a new airport with a larger capacity was absolutely the wrong thing to do.

Both sides dug into their positions resulting in, both literally and figuratively, a Mexican stand off. A team of negotiators was brought in from Harvard. The negotiators found merit in both proposals, allowing both sides to save face, and then said the evidence was not decisive one way or the other. The negotiators suggested that both parties take a five-year moratorium from their positions. During that time the existing airport would be minimally improved. A team of neutral scientists and city planners would re-evaluate the decision in five years' time. If a clear decision could be made to build or not build the new airport, then that decision would be implemented. If a clear decision could not be reached, another five-year moratorium would be put in place.

By providing a creative no-lose solution, the negotiators were able to help both sides in the debate reach an optimal solution. As a result of these efforts, Mexico City has not built a new airport and billions and billions of pesos were saved. Contrast that with the decision to build Mirabel airport outside of Montreal. When it was opened in 1975, Mirabel was one of the most up-to-date airports in the world. The problem was that, for a variety of reasons, no one would use it—millions and millions of taxpayers' dollars were wasted on an airport that no one would use—money that could have been better spent on health care, education, research and development, or on rebuilding the infrastructure. The building and not building of these two airports graphically illustrates the difference between optimal and suboptimal solutions.

INCREASED SAFETY AT NO COST

Like many North American cities, Brantford, Ontario has experienced robberies and associated violence against taxi drivers and against staff who work at convenience stores. The most frequently cited answer was to hire more police to increase protection. However, in times of fiscal restraint this solution was not feasible. It is also questionable whether an increase in the number of police officers will be able to reduce the number of robberies and violence since the police cannot be expected to always be in the right place at the right time.

Paul Kells[1] suggested that by thinking outside the box, the City of Brantford could locate its taxi stands, whenever possible, in front of convenience stores. Through increased surveillance, both taxi drivers and store clerks were better protected, which resulted in fewer incidences of violence against taxi drivers and convenience store personnel.

CANADIAN NATIONAL RAILROAD'S SARNIA-PORT HURON TUNNEL

Increased global competition has affected all aspects of business in Canada. An excellent example of creative thinking was the Canadian National Railroad's plan to double stack its freight cars to save time in addition to shipping and transportation costs.

This is how CN did it. Because of its location, Nova Scotia is one day's sailing closer to Europe than New York is. Goods from Europe unloaded in Halifax can reach Chicago and the American mid-west 24 hours sooner than if they are off-loaded in New York. CN recognized this as a competitive advantage in moving modular containers to the mid-west. CN also knew that it would be much more cost-effective if the containers were double stacked, that is, one container stacked on top of another while sitting on a flatbed railroad car. The Canadian route had fewer tunnels and overpasses than the American one. This was a factor to consider when faced with the modifications that would be needed to accommodate the double-stacked cars.

Even in Canada, it would have been very expensive to redo all of the overpasses and tunnels along the route. Here again thinking outside the box paid off for CN. Instead of modifying the tunnels and overpasses, the tracks were dug several inches deeper, which allowed for the necessary clearance. The last problem was getting the double-stacked trains from Canada to the United States. In order to accomplish this, CN built the Sarnia-Port Huron tunnel under the St. Clair River at a cost of $190 million. "The only link allowing double-stacked railcars to thunder straight through central Canada to the American Midwest."[2] The net result was to increase the container volume, which in terms of portage and stevedoring fees alone, is $20 million. It also created over 800 person years in direct and indirect employment. This has increased the revenue for the Port of Halifax, for Halterm—the company that unloads the containers from the ships and puts them on the trains and trucks—and for CN.

CN could not have negotiated with its customers to obtain a greater share of the freight market without having first developed the creative solutions that gave it these advantages. Thinking outside the box paid off for CN, Halterm and the transportation industry.

HABITAT FOR HUMANITY

There is a tremendously creative project known as Habitat for Humanity, whose purpose is to provide low-cost housing through volunteer material and labour. The way the project is working in Saskatchewan is as follows. Someone has an old building that they would like to have removed. A call is placed to Habitat for Humanity and they carefully dismantle the old building at no cost. The materials are either sold and the proceeds go to charity or the materials are reused to build new buildings in inner cities. Habitat for Humanity also trains aboriginal people in construction, carpentry and building skills in the process. This is a win/win/win/win solution because the old buildings are removed, materials from these buildings are sold or recycled, new buildings in the cities are made more affordable, and a group of deserving people are taught important life and career skills.

THE SAN FRANCISCO AIRPORT CAR RENTAL SHUTTLE BUS PROGRAM

I am sure that most of you have had the experience of flying to a city and renting a car for business or pleasure. If you have, you probably remember waiting for the shuttle bus to pick you up and deliver you to the area where your particular car was reserved. I can also imagine that many of you have been frustrated. The shuttle bus from the company that you rented from always seems to be the last one to come. For example, if you rented from Company "Y," you will see large, almost entirely empty buses for Hertz, Avis, National, Alamo, Dollar, Thrifty, Budget and Tilden pass you by before your particular company's bus finally arrives to pick you up.

It is different at the San Francisco International Airport because eight rental car companies use the same bus to drop off their customers at their combined location. The net result is that the passengers hardly have to wait for a bus, there is 50 percent reduction in air pollution, and over 200,000 gallons of gas is saved per year. This story demonstrates that under the right conditions, even fierce competitors can cooperate to find a win/win solution.

RADICAL CHANGES IN A FIRST NATIONS BAND

I met **Bernd Christmas**, CEO of the Membertou Band, when he was giving a lecture on a leadership development program I teach. Bernd started his presentation by stating that, "My strategy was to confront, head on, the negative stereotype of corrupt bands where funds were misused and the majority of the band members were on welfare." To change the stereotype, he undertook six strategic initiatives.

The First Strategic Initiative

The first strategic initiative was to publish all of the Membertou Band financial statements on the band Web site. "By being this open and transparent, it proves that our band's finances and financial reporting are above reproach."

The Second Strategic Initiative

The second strategic initiative was for the band's governance to be ISO 9000 certified. ISO 9000 certification means that the standards of business under which the band operates must be world class. Certification means that the organization's practices have been inspected on site and meet the stringent standards set out by the International Standards Organization. Recertification must be undertaken every three years. It is also true that many certified organizations will only do business with other organizations that are certified. The Membertou Band will be the first band in the world to be ISO 9000 certified.

The Third Strategic Initiative

The third strategic initiative was to locate the office of the Membertou Corporation in Purdy's Wharf, which is one of the most, if not the most, prestigious locations in downtown Halifax. Bernd Christmas recalls, "My reasoning was that the Membertou Band must go to where the business opportunities are, not wait for business to come to them. All of these initiatives have reached a critical mass. The Membertou Corporation has now won contracts worth tens of millions of dollars."

The Fourth Strategic Initiative

Hire the best. This hire the best strategy started with Chief Terry Paul when he convinced Bernd Christmas to leave his corporate legal practice in Toronto and become the lawyer for and CEO of the Membertou Corporation. A major recruiting drive was then aimed towards members working away from the community;

> *My reasoning was that the Membertou Band must go to where the business opportunities are, not wait for business to come to them.*
>
> **Bernd Christmas**

and subsequently, individuals in senior positions, both in the private and public sector, were hired. The Membertou Development Corporation currently has a strong management team having recruited members from Mobil/Exxon, Deloitte & Touche, Health Canada, Nestlé, Revenue Canada and the Union of Nova Scotia Indians.

The Fifth Strategic Initiative

The fifth strategic initiative was to reinforce that the Membertou office was a place of work first, socialization second. Bernd comments, "In the past, the band office was the centre of social life on the reserve. As a result, members of the community dropped in at any time for a cup of coffee, to hear the latest band and/or member news. As a result essential band work was not being done and the strategic initiatives were not advancing at the rate they needed to."

B.M. *How did you overcome these problems?*

B.C. The first change was to remove the chairs from the lobby and the last pot of coffee was made at 3:00 P.M. The second change was that if anyone wanted to talk with any of the people who worked in the band office, they had to go through the receptionist first.

Our ultimate goal was to balance the best of the Mi'kmaw culture with the best of the western culture. In order to achieve this balance, one more strategic initiative had to be put into place.

The Sixth Strategic Initiative

The fifth initiative led directly into the sixth: "We have started the first total immersion program in the Mi'kmaw language and culture and the Membertou Band has taken over the responsibility for the education of its children from the provincial government."

In summary, Bernd Christmas is a leader, visionary and negotiator worth watching. His six strategic stereotype-busting initiatives have not only radically changed the way the business community views the Membertou Band, but also the way the Membertou Band and its members view themselves.

INNOVATION AND A NEW KIND OF FINANCIAL INSTITUTION

Innovative changes were at the heart of establishing Vancouver City Savings Credit Union (VanCity) as a new kind of financial institute in British Columbia. The following interview with **Dave Mowat**, president of VanCity illustrates that the need for outside-the-box thinking continues to be mandatory in today's hyper-competitive financial marketplace.

B.M. *Can you give me an example that best illustrates the use of creative, out-of-the-box thinking at VanCity?*

D.M. Twenty-five years ago, we chose GEAC to develop our customer financial statement reporting system. To this very day the other financial institutions would love to do what we do. Our system allows us to develop an "All In One" statement. This means that everything is on one statement. In other words, VanCity customers can see their chequing account balance, saving account balance, mortgage, car loan, boat loan, etc. all on one statement and this is one of the ways that we provide excellent customer member service.

> *We have always had a keen, strategic interest in technology. We launched our own home-banking program over the Internet a year before any of the other Canadian banks.*
>
> **Dave Mowat**

We have always had a keen, strategic interest in technology. We launched our own home-banking program over the Internet a year before any of the other Canadian banks.

We have also launched Citizens Bank on PC and TV across Canada. Many people ask us why we are still in TV banking when only 200 people use that version. The reason is future convergence between television and the computer. Lastly, we have plans to use video conferencing so you can speak to a teller over the Internet if you want to.

WHAT DO THESE SEVEN CREATIVE SOLUTIONS HAVE IN COMMON?

The first thing that these creative solutions have in common is the ability to think outside the box. It is not enough, however, to have a good or even great idea, you have to influence others in order to carry out and be committed to implement those ideas. If we use our IQ to help us think up the creative ideas, then we need our EQ (Emotional Intelligence) in order to effectively implement them.

Thinking Outside the Box

Innovation, flexibility and thinking outside the box are important tools for all negotiators and problem solvers. Fortunately, these are learnable skills. If you find negotiations are at an impasse, there are six methods that can help you in thinking outside the box.

1. Look at past creative solutions and see which elements of those solutions might transfer to a current situation.

2. Consult with other creative thinkers.

3. Read about as many creative solutions as you can and make a list of the most creative that were used.

4. Process other examples of creative solutions and follow the reasoning backwards to identify the mental models used to generate those creative solutions.

5. Learn how to use enhanced brainstorming.

6. Keep a creative solutions log. You will be surprised at how often examples in your log can help you think outside the box.

LOOK AT PAST CREATIVE SOLUTIONS

I found the perfect example of this principle when I interviewed **Neville Gilfoy**, the president and publisher of *Atlantic Progress* magazine. In today's hyper-competitive market, publishing magazines is one of the most difficult undertakings anyone can choose. One of the reasons for *Atlantic Progress'* success is Neville's ability to think outside the box, as the following example demonstrates.

Atlantic Progress is a magazine that focuses on business, entrepreneurial and political issues that affect business in Atlantic Canada. Like most magazines, *Atlantic Progress* depends on revenues generated through advertising. Not surprisingly, the September issue was notoriously difficult to sell advertising for because the two months prior, July and August, are generally the time when most people are on vacation. Neville reframed the problem as to what would have to happen to make the September issue not only the most popular issue, but also the one that sold the most advertisements and brought in the most revenue. The solution to this seemingly impossible problem was to publish "The Top 101 Companies in Atlantic Canada" in the September issue. Naturally, everyone wanted to see how their company and their competitors ranked. The September issue is now *Atlantic Progress'* largest, as well as most profitable, seller.

Not one to underutilize a good idea, *Atlantic Progress* also publishes "The 100 Fastest Growing Companies in Atlantic Canada" in March and plans to launch an edition that features "The 100 Best Companies to Work for in Atlantic Canada."

The next time you get stuck trying to find the answer to a difficult problem, think of previous solutions to other seemingly difficult problems and see if elements of those solutions can be applied to the present situation.

CONSULT WITH OTHER CREATIVE THINKERS

We all become habituated to looking at a problem in the same way, and sometimes we just cannot see our way out of the self-imposed boundaries we place on a particular problem. For example, each of us has lost a pair of glasses or a set of keys. We turn the house upside down but still cannot find the lost item anywhere. We ask another person to have a quick look for us, and within a short period of time, the person finds the missing item for us. The ability to look at a problem from a fresh perspective is often the key to solving apparently unsolvable problems. I asked **Paul Tellier** about this.

> *In any negotiation it's team work, and all negotiators are only as good as the team that they have in place.*
>
> **Paul Tellier**

B.M. *What is the importance of fresh perspectives?*

P.T. In my work over the last 25 years I have always had someone who was a great debriefer—a close colleague with whom I could interface on a regular basis. The first guy I brought in when I came to CN was Michael Sabia [chief financial officer].[3] We would discuss important issues on a daily basis. He would tell me, "What you said yesterday was basically wrong for the following reasons," and we would challenge and debate one another. In any negotiation it's team work, and all negotiators are only as good as the team that they have in place.

ACTIVELY SEEK OUT CREATIVE SOLUTIONS

Read about as many creative solutions as you can and make a list of the most creative that were used. I have studied at Harvard and read most of the books published by the Harvard Program on Negotiation. They contain many wonderful examples of creative solutions. Other excellent sources of creative solutions are the books on *Emotional Intelligence* by Daniel Goleman. These books, and many more, are listed in the Resources from the Masters: An Annotated Bibliography.

IDENTIFY MENTAL MODELS USED TO GENERATE CREATIVE SOLUTIONS

One of the creative solutions that was put forward at the Harvard Program for Negotiation to help resolve the Major League Baseball strike, which lasted for 232 days in 1994 and 1995, was to have a "virtual strike." In a virtual strike, the players would continue to play, but would receive only enough money to cover their expenses. Likewise, the owners of the ball teams would continue to receive enough money to cover their expenses. A neutral bank would hold all of the extra money. Every day that the players and owners did not settle, an increasingly large amount of the money that was put into escrow would be turned over to charity. For example, by the time $50 million had been accumulated—half of which would be turned over to charity—there would be a tremendous amount of pressure on both sides to settle.

One way to learn how to find similar creative solutions in the future is by working backwards to try to figure out how other problem solvers arrived at the solutions to their problems. In the baseball example, as the original situation unfolded, both the players and the owners came to appear more and more greedy to the general public. The opposite of greed is charity. Therefore, the creators of this solution needed to look for a solution that had being charitable at its heart. In other words, how could the negative impression of being greedy be reframed positively? Therefore, reframing negatives into positives is one of the methods that can be used to help invent creative solutions.

Use Enhanced Brainstorming

We have all used brainstorming successfully to help us think outside the box. The ground rules for brainstorming are that we have a set period of time, for example, the next half-hour, to say any idea that comes into our minds with absolutely no criticism. Often an idea that seems ill-conceived may be an innovative solution to a problem, may lead to an innovative idea or may be combined with other ideas to help resolve a problem. Two innovative procedures that can help enhance the traditional ground rules of brainstorming are as follows.

Firstly, even though we know the ground rules, many times we silently criticize someone else's suggestion. One way to get around this natural tendency is to ask the other parties involved to come up with different ways to make someone else's suggestion work, rather than to think about ways that it would not work. Once again, no criticism is allowed in the brainstorming process. This procedure helps us use brainstorming not only in the generation of ideas, but also in the implementation of ideas.

The second method is a high-tech solution to the problem of giving more or less weight to ideas based on who generated the ideas or the status they hold. For example, in some parts of the Canadian military they conduct brainstorming sessions via e-mail. This way, a colonel's ideas are given the same weight as a private's. No one knows whose idea it is, which helps to insure that all of the ideas are adequately considered.

Keep a Creative Solutions Log

People who are good at telling jokes keep a list of materials from which to draw. They also practise telling jokes, and learn how to use the right word and the right pause at the right time. Just as joke telling is a learned art, so is learning to think outside the box in creative problem solving. By keeping a creative solutions log in which you keep a description of the creative solutions and/or the mental models used to arrive at creative solutions, and consulting it the next time you find that you are stuck in a box, you will be surprised at how often examples in your log can help you think outside the box. Exercises 1-1 and 1-2 could be the start of your own creative solutions log.

EXERCISE 1-1

Observing Creative Solutions

In the space below, outline three creative solutions that you have seen but that did not originate with you.

1. _____
   _____
   _____
   _____
   _____
   _____
   _____

2. _____
   _____
   _____
   _____
   _____
   _____
   _____

3. _____
   _____
   _____
   _____
   _____
   _____
   _____

EXERCISE 1-2

Your Own Creative Solutions

In the space below, list three creative solutions that you thought of.

1. _____

   _____

   _____

   _____

   _____

   _____

   _____

2. _____

   _____

   _____

   _____

   _____

   _____

   _____

3. _____

   _____

   _____

   _____

   _____

   _____

   _____

   _____

Turn Your Vision into a Compelling Advantage

When I began writing this book, I added a section on vision and negotiating but was not sure how appropriate it was until I started my interviews with Master Canadian Negotiators. In each instance, their vision acted as a compass in helping them overcome large obstacles, by increasing their commitment, and in bringing their projects to fruition.

For example, one of the most important negotiations in the life of an organization is the negotiation to re-position that organization. Re-positioning an organization is successful under five conditions:

1. a looming or imminent crisis;
2. an inherent opportunity;
3. a compelling and concrete vision of a vastly superior future state;
4. the ability to recruit a critical number of others in the organization to champion the vision; and
5. sustained leadership in order to overcome each and every obstacle so that the compelling vision can be implemented.

Most organizations fail in their attempts to re-position themselves because only one, or at most two, of these conditions is present.

In this section I will summarize two Canadian cases that exemplify these five critical steps in organizational realignment. The first case is the amalgamation of five Montreal hospitals into the McGill University Health Centre. The second case is the merging of the four Atlantic Canadian telephone companies into one company, Aliant Inc.

THE McGILL UNIVERSITY HEATH CENTRE

Health care is one of the biggest political issues in both Canada and the United States. Health care costs are rising exponentially, taking a larger and larger piece of each province's overall budget. The baby boom generation is aging so there will be more and more demands placed on the ailing health care system. At the same time, medicine is advancing at the fastest rate ever. Every day sees new and important medical breakthroughs, all of which cost significant amounts of money. How to balance medical costs and patients' needs, and fund medical research are some of the most important economic and political questions of our times.

Enter **Dr. Nicolas Steinmetz**, executive director of the Montreal Children's Hospital. In early 1992, five Montreal hospitals—the Montreal Children's, Montreal General, Montreal Neurological, Montreal Chest and the Royal Victoria Hospitals—were facing a common dilemma. Their physical infrastructure was deteriorating and they each needed a critical amount of funding in order to maintain their world-renowned reputations for patient care, research and teaching. Hospitals and their boards are notoriously territorial. The Montreal hospitals had world-class reputations and were fiercely proud institutions. Under Dr. Steinmetz's leadership, a study was carried out to consider two alternatives: the cost of up-grading each hospital's present facilities, or building a new facility that would house all five hospitals.

Like all Master Negotiators, Dr. Steinmetz was well-prepared to argue the merits of building the new complex. The projected costs of upgrading the existing hospitals were over $300 million. In one hospital alone, the cost of upgrading for fire safety was $12 million. The cost of building a new complex was $1.3 billion. However, the operational savings at the new complex were projected to be over $40 million per year.

Based on the results of this study, on March 31, 1994, these five teaching hospitals of McGill University signed a Memorandum of Understanding to begin planning the creation of the McGill University Health Centre (MUHC). To date, the planning department of MUHC has studied the most modern teaching hospitals in the world. They have also conducted numerous planning sessions in order to get input from all of the various stakeholders such as: doctors, nurses, patients, medical researchers, teaching faculty and community members.

The vision for the new MUHC is electrifying. The challenge is to envision an environment that is not only the most technologically advanced, but also the most supportive of patients' own healing processes. Construction of the hospital is planned to begin in 2003 and to be finished by the end of 2005. Part of the vision is to take advantage of the economies of scale in that five hospitals will be together on one site. The planners also have to predict and get expert advice on how to maximize the use of technology and informatics; how to design state-of-the-art laboratories; how advances in medicine will contribute to more day surgery or other, non-invasive treatments; and how to design the hospital complex so that patients will receive state-of-the-art care with minimal discomfort and maximum privacy. The design of the hospital will take into account the growing body of research on the effects that the building environment has on patient care outcomes. This will include such variables as light, temperature, ventilation, colour, sound/noise and aromas.

The primary vision for the MUHC is to enable the McGill University Faculty of Medicine to maintain and enhance its outstanding achievements as a world-class centre of excellence in research, teaching and patient care at the new facility. There will also be a strong focus on maximizing the cross-fertilization between basic science and medical science, which will contribute to the advancement of both.

My words and understanding of all of these complex issues are not adequate to describe the excitement and potential of this project. Unsolicited comments from the staff that I worked with described their work at the MUHC as a once-in-a-lifetime learning experience.

The question I have is this: Would the opportunity to build one of the most modern and innovative hospitals in the world have occurred without the vision of Dr. Nicolas Steinmetz? The answer is clearly no. It also would not have happened without the use of objective criteria, for instance, the cost comparisons of repairing, upgrading and maintaining the five existing hospitals versus the cost and opportunity of starting from scratch.

We now turn to our second example of how vision is being used to lead a very different type of organization into the future.

MERGING OF THE FOUR ATLANTIC CANADIAN
TELEPHONE COMPANIES

Deregulation changed forever the way communication companies—MTT in Nova Scotia, Island Tel in Prince Edward Island, NewTel in Newfoundland, and NBTel in New Brunswick—ran their respective businesses. For the first time, there was competition, in fact, fierce competition, for long distance customers. It seemed like every day there was a new long distance plan and, for far too many evenings, my telephone rang with one or another long distance carrier trying to get my business. In addition to competition from other long distance carriers, there is also competition from cable companies to deliver phone services. As well, vastly expensive new technologies are being developed and introduced: fibre optics, Internet service, cell phone and broadband data pipes. Telephone company employees who were participants in one of my change management workshops described the changes that were introduced with deregulation at their phone company as follows. I asked the participants to form into small groups of five. Their task was to make a drawing of the way the telephone company had been and to make a drawing of the current state. Their drawing of the past depicted the telephone company as a Boeing 747 aircraft—utterly stable and predictable. It took off in Vancouver, flew to Toronto, and returned. They described post deregulation as being on the U.S.S. Enterprise, being attacked by the Klingons and not being sure which galaxy they were headed for.

More recently, the four Atlantic telephone companies merged into one company, Aliant Inc. During the transition, each company kept its individual identity as more and more functions were merged over time.

A compelling vision was needed to bring these independent and previously competitive companies together into a unified whole. An important part of this vision was developed by **David Rathbun**, chief human resources officer.

David's vision is that to be a viable and competitive world-class organization, Aliant has to be a learning organization—not just in lip service, but also in actual fact. Human resources will be made up of four components, Aliant

Learning, Aliant Career, Aliant Excellence and Aliant Compensation. The reason for the four components is that each component will have a department head whose job it is to champion the function of that department. David had three critical areas of his vision that came up during our interview:

1. that Aliant must be a learning organization;
2. that Aliant must be highly collaborative; and
3. that Aliant must develop its human resources through high-level individual and group coaching.

Create a Learning Organization

B.M. *What is your vision for Aliant and how will this vision help in the negotiations to bring these four companies together?*

D.R. Our vision for Aliant is to be a world-class global organization that is results-oriented. One of the specific results that we will achieve is to double our revenue by 2003. Because of our mandate to grow, we will be subject to rapid and diverse growth. Aliant must, therefore, be nimble and adapt quickly. We can only do that by having a work force that is constantly developing new skills.

To be globally competitive we must have the best-trained and most highly skilled workers so we can take full advantage of every opportunity in both our mature and our emerging business. Our mandate is to understand the learning needs of our organization two to three years in the future, to hire and train the best talent possible while constantly developing our current talent. We will constantly undertake gap analyses of the skills that will be necessary two to three years in the future and then design and/or buy the skill development programs that are necessary for us to help our staff learn and enhance their skills and competencies so we can take advantage of all of the opportunities the new economy has to offer.

Aliant will also hire a CLO (chief learning officer). The role of the CLO is to be a builder of bridges, *i.e.*, to bridge our workforce to the organization's future needs, and to be a highly visible champion of learning. The CLO's role is to send a strong signal that Aliant is a learning organization to our employees [and] to our customers and that Aliant will be perceived as a true learning organization by all members of the external community.

> *Our mandate is to understand the learning needs of our organization two to three years in the future, to hire and train the best talent possible while constantly developing our current talent.*
>
> **David Rathbun**

Use Internal Collaboration

B.M. *Tell me about your plans to increase internal collaboration.*

D.R. While there is no shortage of external competition, internal competition can cripple most organizations which is why having a shared vision is so important. Therefore, all of our business units have to learn to work together collaboratively in order to develop the synergy that is necessary to be world-class. We will also be spending more time partnering [and hence negotiating] with other organizations to develop and implement product systems that none of us could achieve individually.

As Peter F. Drucker states "Organizations are no longer built on force. They are increasingly built on trust."[4] Without collaboration there can be no trust, and without trust, there can be no collaboration. Therefore, teaching staff how to negotiate collaboratively is one of the most important learning objectives at Aliant.

An example of this type of effective collaboration is the Integrated Wide Area Network (IWAN) Project. The IWAN Project is designed to bring state-of-the-art radio communication to the province of Nova Scotia. The partners are MTT, the province of Nova Scotia and Motorola. As a result of this project and by working together collaboratively, Nova Scotia will have one of the world's most up-to-date dispatch systems to coordinate the activities of ambulance, police and fire services. This system will help to save lives during times of emergency.

Develop Human Resources through Individual and Group Coaching

There must be a great deal of effort put into high-level coaching in order to develop our best performers. In this regard, David Rathbun buys into Peter Drucker's dictum to:

> . . . waste as little effort as possible on improving areas of low competence. Concentration should be on areas of high competence and high skills. It takes far more energy and far more work to improve from incompetence to low mediocrity than it takes to improve from first-rate performance to excellence. And yet most . . . organizations . . . try to concentrate on making an incompetent person into a low mediocrity. The energy and resources—and time—should instead go into making a competent person into a star performer.[5]

Why Does the Word "Vision" Have Such a Bad Name?

Most people do not differentiate between developing and writing a vision and living one. Permit me to give two examples that illustrate the difference between a "dead" and a "living" vision. When my father was dying of lung cancer in California, he was admitted to a gorgeous new hospital in the San Francisco Bay area. In fact, in terms of design, furnishings and landscaping, the hospital resembled a first-class hotel. There was a beautifully written mission statement in a gold frame opposite the elevators on each floor. Yet many times when we arrived to visit, we found that the staff had neglected him. With the help of home hospice, he was brought home where he received first-class care. Contrast this to the old Grace Maternity Hospital in Halifax, Nova Scotia, where my children were born. At that time, the Grace was literally falling apart. There was so little room that medical equipment lined the walls of all the hallways. If there was a written mission statement for the hospital, I did not see one. Yet, one of the first things our delivery nurse said to us was that we were smart to choose the Grace for the birth of our child because the Grace had the highest live delivery rate of any hospital in North America. For me, this is one of the best examples of a "living" mission statement. If your staff cannot summarize your organization's mission statement in three to seven words, your mission statement has little or no impact.

DEVELOP YOUR OWN VISION AND ENHANCE YOUR NEGOTIATING ABILITY

Master Negotiators embody the strong relation between vision, commitment, building strategic alliances and the expert use of negotiation and influencing strategies that are necessary to move a vision closer to reality. From Bernd Christmas' goal to confront Native stereotypes to David Rathbun's vision of Aliant Inc. as a world class learning organization, to Dr. Nicholas Steinmetz's undertaking of building a state-of-the-art teaching hospital, the Master Negotiators we have met so far have aptly illustrated the powerful roles of vision and commitment in effective negotiating strategies. The following section has been designed to help the reader develop and enhance their own vision, whether that vision is for their professional life, personal life, or both.

Harold Taylor is a certified speaking professional and one of a select group of people who have been inducted into the Canadian Association of Professional Speakers' Hall of Fame. He is also one of North America's leading experts in time management, having written 13 books and hundreds of articles.

B.M. *Harold, what role does vision play in your life and career?*

H.T My vision is to help individuals and organizations manage their time, achieve their goals and manage their lives as effectively as possible through workshops, presentations, products, publications and personal example.

When I discovered that disorganization was a common affliction among individuals and organizations alike, I decided to make it my career. There were hundreds of trainers and speakers in Canada who conducted time management seminars, among other things. But I knew of no one who provided time management workshops and presentations to the exclusion of everything else.

I visualized myself being the top authority in time management in Canada and immediately set a time frame of 10 years in which to make this happen. Among the questions that I had to answer for myself were: "How would a time management expert behave? What would their promotional materials look like? What would they have accomplished?"

I knew I had to publish articles, even if I had to pay to get them into print. I had to write a book, even if I had to publish it myself. I had to write a monthly newsletter, even if there were only one subscriber. I had to be interviewed on radio and TV, speak to large audiences, and create something new in the field of time management. My efforts during the early years were not focused on making large profits but on gaining visibility and recognition as Canada's leading authority in the field of time management.

I declined all speaking engagements scheduled on Sundays, accepted only one Saturday per month and two evenings per month. People soon got the idea that I was in control of my time, and practised what I preached.

I turned down speaking engagements outside my chosen field even though I could have used the money. I used the time to read and write and study and develop products and programs. I didn't just read books; I bought them. Anyone can claim to have read over 700 books on time management. But actually seeing them cover an entire office wall raises credibility. It's not enough to say you're an expert; you must build physical evidence that you are an expert. I was able to *negotiate* [emphasis added] from a perceived strength when talking to potential clients.

Twenty years have passed since I had the vision of being Canada's top authority on time management. I have written 13 books, hundreds of articles, and developed over 50 time management products. My newsletter is now in its twenty-first year of publication. My Web site sells products to 36 countries. I now have associates facilitating my workshops.

> *I visualized myself being the top authority in time management in Canada and immediately set a time frame of 10 years in which to make this happen.*
>
> **Harold Taylor**

Today, Harold Taylor is recognized to be the expert on time management in both Canada and the United States. Harold's story richly illustrates the importance of how vision, preparation, commitment and focus contribute to one's ability to negotiate as effectively as possible. All of the Master Negotiators that I have met have discovered this powerful combination, as their subsequent stories in this book will attest.

Exercises 1-3 to 1-6 are designed to help you develop a clearer vision for yourself regardless of whether it is a personal vision, a professional vision or both.

EXERCISE 1-3

Your Vision Statement

Write a vision statement for your job, team, department, organization or your personal life.

_____

_____

_____

_____

_____

_____

_____

_____

_____

_____

_____

_____

_____

_____

_____

_____

_____

_____

_____

_____

EXERCISE 1-4

Vision Statement Feedback

List three people whom you could interview as to how they see your personal and/or professional vision.

1. _____

2. _____

3. _____

Master Negotiators know the importance of salient feedback. Ask carefully selected people who know you well and who will be absolutely honest with you on how they see your personal or professional vision. Their feedback may surprise you. They may see your vision more clearly and interpret it more articulately than you do. Secondly, ask them how they see your behaviour as being both congruent and incongruent with your vision.

_____
_____
_____
_____
_____
_____
_____
_____
_____
_____
_____
_____

From *The Seven Strategies of Master Negotiators* by Brad McRae © 2002, McGraw-Hill Ryerson.

EXERCISE 1-5

Envision Your Future

Draw a picture of the way you currently see yourself and then a second picture of how you would like to see yourself at some time in the future, for example in five years' time.

I have used Exercise 1-5 hundreds of times with both individual and corporate clients. There is almost always a tendency to make this exercise harder than it is by doubting one's ability to draw, however, once you try it, you will find this exercise to be very rewarding. The second advantage of Exercise 1-5 is that it almost always either brings up new and valuable information or it presents information we already know in a larger and more useful context.

The following example from one of my workshop participants illustrates the power of this technique. Mike is a very hard-working entrepreneur who has his own company that sells several lines of top quality cameras and camera equipment to retail stores. Mike attended one of my time management workshops and one of the exercises he completed was Exercise 1-5. Mike approached me at the end of the workshop to share with me how powerful this exercise had been for him. Mike said:

> I have known for a long time that I both wanted to and should be spending more time with my family, but I always had a good excuse because of this or that business commitment. What amazed me about this exercise, was that in the ideal state, I had drawn pictures of myself spending more time with my wife and children, with business and recreation filling up the more peripheral parts of the drawing. Somehow, seeing it, rather than thinking it had a much more powerful impact on me and I intend to do something about it!

Firstly, one of the results of completing Exercise 1-6—the letter to the future—and from doing Exercises 1-3 to 1-6, is a more vivid and detailed description of your vision for your personal life, professional life or both. Secondly, the outcome of Exercises 1-3 through 1-6 will act as a magnet drawing you to it.

EXERCISE 1-6

Write a Letter to the Future[5]

Chose a time in the future—5, 10, 15 years from now, or any longer or shorter amount of time that is meaningful to you. Write the imaginary future date at the top of the letter, for example, July 28, 2010. Imagine that the intervening years have passed and that you are writing to a close friend and confidant. Use the friend's name in the salutation, as in, "Dear [friend's name]," or if you prefer, pick some other supportive person to whom you can comfortably imagine writing. The purpose of dating the letter and writing it to someone you actually know is to strengthen the psychological realism of the letter.

It is common at this stage for your mind to go into cognitive meltdown at the prospect of writing about the future in the past tense. The best thing to do here is to thank your mind for sharing and do it anyway. After the initial discomfort, it becomes much easier.

Imagine that in this future you have creatively resolved any current problems, transitions, and/or uncertainty in your life. Describe the creative solutions that helped you to resolve those problems. At the time of the letter writing, you are living a wonderful, joyous, healthy and satisfying life. Describe how you are spending your time, where you are living, your relationships, beliefs and reflections on the past and future.

From *The Seven Strategies of Master Negotiators* by Brad McRae © 2002, McGraw-Hill Ryerson.

In conclusion, Master Negotiators develop a clear vision of the future based on creative rather than wasteful solutions, they have learned the skill of thinking outside the box, and they actively seek creative ideas from others. But having the vision by itself is not enough. After developing a vision based on creative rather than wasteful solutions, Master Negotiators ensure that they come to the table incredibly well-prepared, which is the second strategy that Master Negotiators use to bring their vision closer to reality.

---

[1] Founder and vice-chair of the Safe Communities Foundation. Paul has turned the tragic workplace death of his son, Sean, into a call for action on eliminating workplace injuries and improving the health and safety of people across the country. See: **www.safecommunities.ca.**

[2] Harry Bruce. *The Pig that Flew: the Battle to Privatize Canadian National.* Vancouver, B.C.: Douglas & McIntyre, 1997, at p. 25.

[3] Michael Sabia became the president of Bell Canada Enterprises in December 2000.

[4] *Management Challenges for the 21st Century.* New York: HarperBusiness, 1999, at p. 187.

[5] Ibid., at p. 168.

STRATEGY 2

Come to the Table
Incredibly Well-Prepared

"Master Negotiators come to the table incredibly well-prepared, while their amateur counterparts come to the table overly confident and under prepared."

— *Brad McRae*

One of the most unusual and innovative stories I have heard about the power of preparation was from a workshop participant named Peter. I met Peter when I was doing a negotiation workshop for Pete's Tire Barn, in western Massachusetts. Peter was a sales representative whose job it was to sell truck tires. Most people do not know it, but after the purchase of the truck, tires are a trucker's second most expensive purchase. It is important for the trucking firm to have the right tire on their trucks in terms of safety, fuel economy and tire longevity.

Peter explained how he used the power of preparation to be one-up on his competition. He said that while most of the other truck tire sales representatives would spend their Sundays watching football and other sporting events on television, he would be out doing his preparatory research by looking through his customers' and potential customers' garbage bins. I couldn't resist—I had to ask him why. Peter told me that he often found discarded truck tires in the garbage bins. He would then study the discarded tires to find out if they had been discarded because of natural aging, or if the firm was using the wrong type of tires for its vehicles. He could make an informed recommendation to the trucking firm as to how one of his tires could do a better job. For me, this story captures the power of preparation and it also explains why Peter of Pete's Tire Barn was one of the best truck tire salesmen in North America.

While most of the other truck tire sales representatives would spend their Sundays watching football and other sporting events on television, Peter would be out doing his preparatory research by looking through his customers' and potential customers' garbage bins.

Peter's method of preparation is not for everyone, but it illustrates how preparation can give you an added advantage at the negotiating table. There are a number of ways you can better prepare for negotiating including:

1. surface and validate assumptions;
2. be realistic about what you can accomplish;
3. develop and use concrete examples to help make your point;
4. have the best BATNA to gain the stronger negotiating position;
5. be prepared, but be flexible;
6. expect the unexpected;
7. use role play to augment your preparation;
8. present your case using objective criteria;
9. determine your leverage;
10. write down possible trade offs or concessions.

It is one thing to know about the importance of these points and skills, and yet another to use them correctly. The first part of this chapter examines these skills and techniques in detail. The last part of the chapter will introduce you to the Master Negotiators' Preparation Form (Figure 2-1). By using the form you can make sure that you are as prepared as the Master Negotiators I interviewed in this book.

Surface and Validate Assumptions

The following story illustrates the importance of surfacing and validating assumptions. I had just gotten out of a relaxing sauna at our local gym after having had a work out. I was starting to shave at the sink, when I felt a horrific stabbing pain go through my right foot. I involuntarily screamed and looked down to see a tan coloured steel-toed Kodiak boot being removed from my still aching foot. I was about to turn around and tell the boot's owner what I thought of his clumsiness, when I noticed, to my total chagrin, that the man was blind. Luckily, I hadn't said anything, but I can tell you that I felt all of two inches tall.

Assumptions are a vital part of our everyday lives and save us an incredible amount of time and energy. Each day we make thousands of decisions, some good, some with no effect, and some with very poor outcomes. Each decision that we make is based on, to a greater or lesser degree, the assumptions that validate that decision.

The difference between Master Negotiators and their amateur counterparts is that for Master Negotiators, it is not acceptable to keep making faulty assumptions and continue to generate sub-optimal solutions. In fact, the biggest mistake that amateur negotiators make is coming to the table overly optimistic and under prepared, as the following story by Master Negotiator **Bill Black** so richly illustrates. Bill Black has been president of Maritime Life since 1995. This story illustrates that by being well-prepared, by understanding the negotiating process and by persevering, Bill negotiated a successful deal that essentially doubled the size of his company.

B.M. *Tell me about Maritime Life's acquisition of Aetna.*

B.B. The Aetna Insurance Company was put up for sale in 1999. The way the process works is that the company that is for sale hires an auctioneer who collects the bids. In the end, there were two very competitive bids and we found out that we [at Maritime Life] were neck and neck with another major national insurance company. At what we thought was the end of the process, I got a call from the auctioneer saying that we were not the successful bidder. It was then up to me to tell a very disappointed team that we had lost.

While the lawyers from Aetna and the other insurance company were black lining the final agreement [putting the final agreement into words], a disagreement arose over two issues. The other insurance company decided to hold firm on the two issues.

The next week, the auctioneer phoned Maritime Life to see if we were interested in improving our previous bid, *and* he needed to know immediately. I was somewhere up in the air on a plane between Boston and Halifax and it was impossible to get hold of me. The team decided to go for it. I was not only pleased with its decision, but also with the fact that the team felt empowered to make that decision without my input.

We now had a small window of opportunity to get back in there. I started calling people at 8 A.M. Saturday. We had 20 people here by 9 A.M. By noon it became evident that we couldn't do it in time. I said to call in more people. By 2 P.M., we had 65 people working on our new bid and by 6 P.M. that night we were done. On Sunday morning a dozen of us set out on a plane and went to the auctioneer's boardroom in Toronto and by 9 P.M. Sunday night we had the deal.

It was amazing that we had this little window and we got in there. The lawyers on both sides, the auctioneer's and our own, were very good. They knew that they were there to paper the deal and the lawyers on both sides were very reasonable. The funny thing was, that while we were working on our revised bid, we were told that the legal team from the other insurance company was out celebrating their "victory."

This story beautifully illustrates the first rule of effective negotiating: professional negotiators go into their negotiations incredibly well-prepared while amateur negotiators go into their negotiations overly confident and under prepared. If Maritime Life had not been well-prepared they could never have made a new bid in such a short time frame. And their competitor's assumption that they had won the bid opened the door to give Maritime a second chance. To this rule, Bill added three others:

1. We are not allowed to be tired.
2. We are not allowed to get excited.
3. We are not allowed to get annoyed.

I was hooked, I had to find out what he meant by his three additional rules.

B.M. *Can you expand on your rules?*

B.B. The reason I said that you are not allowed to be tired is because the type of negotiations I am thinking about are not like sprints, they are like marathons. Therefore it is essential that the participants have to learn to pace themselves. Learning how to pace yourself is purely intuitive, you learn that each negotiation has a pace and rhythm of its own. As well, you have to imagine hurdles that may or may not come up. It is also important to know how the time card is being played, and never let the time card work against you. I have seen the time card force people to give in on items of great substance because they were running out of time. Never let the time card work against you.

The second rule is that we are not allowed to get excited. As the above story illustrates, the other bidder got excited, they had thought that they had won [and] that the time had run out [for us].

B.M.   *In other words, negotiation is much like surgery, the surgeon cannot lose even one second of concentration, by being too optimistic or by being too pessimistic.*

B.B.   The third rule is never allow yourself to be annoyed. Only use emotion and display it if you have a specific purpose. It almost never helps to have an emotional barrier between yourself and the person you are negotiating with. Firstly, if they lose face because of your outburst, they may never forgive you and there is a strong tendency to want to get even—even if it takes years. Secondly, having an outburst also causes a break in focus.

There is an interesting statistic that one-third of all auto accidents occur when people are angry. We don't want the negotiation highway littered with accidents because we allowed ourselves to be annoyed.

B.M.   *How did you develop these rules?*

B.B.   Experience, you do lots of bids, you get some, you don't get some, but you always debrief. I remember that after one of the first bids we didn't get, I asked the auctioneer for very specific feedback; I told her that I was new at this and that I sincerely wanted to learn from my mistakes. One of the things that she told me was that the one who gets the deal is the one who is still sitting at the table after everyone else has left. That was the starting point for those three rules.

There were a number of additional rules that Bill mentioned in the interview.

> *You learn that each negotiation has a pace and a rhythm of its own*
>
> **Bill Black**

- Always get feedback as to how well you negotiated—learn from your successful negotiations and from your failures
- It's not over till it's over
- Be quiet and listen (I can't tell you the number of times that I have negotiated successfully by saying nothing)
- Always treat the other person with respect
- Try to make sure you agree early on the data
- Look for mutual goals for convergence
- You have to be willing to stand up and walk away
- People speak in code, listen to the code

Be Realistic

Major-General Lewis MacKenzie was the Commander of the United Nations Protection Force in Bosnia-Herzegovina from March 9 to August 2, 1992, during the horrifying civil war between the Bosnian Serbs, Croats and Muslims. He spoke eloquently about the role of preparation for his negotiations in Bosnia, and for the future of United Nations' peacekeeping operations.

B.M. *Major-General MacKenzie, what was your vision for your role in Bosnia?*

L.M. Vision is dictated by mandate, however, I interpreted it somewhat more broadly than the Security Council wanted. I saw my role as making sure that the food and medicine would get delivered, even though I knew a lot of it would end up on the black market. I also saw my role as maintaining contact with all sides in the dispute and using the good offices of the United Nations as a neutral place where negotiations could take place. I also wanted to alleviate the situation in Sarajevo by trying to reduce the shelling and sniping as much as possible.

Opening the Sarajevo Airport was critical not only to bring in medicines and other badly needed supplies, it was also an important symbolic victory. Restoring the airport could be seen as the beginning of the restoration of a "civil society" in Bosnia-Herzegovina. At the same time, as a negotiator, MacKenzie was realistic about what could be accomplished and the resources it would take to rebuild a civil society in that war-torn country.

B.M. *What is your vision for peacekeeping since your retirement from active duty?*

L.M. I see my role now as working hard to convince Canadians and the Canadian government of the importance of peacekeeping and to help educate the United Nations and governments around the world of the importance of peacekeeping and peace enforcement. Peace-keeping takes well equipped and well trained troops. Asking a country to sacrifice their sons and daughters, where they are not adequately prepared or equipped for modern-day peacekeeping is not acceptable. The United Nations cannot assume that member countries can or will send in troops that are well-prepared. Therefore, before sending in troops, it is necessary to *verify* that they are both well trained and well equipped. Without doing this, we are asking for failure.

It is also essential that we repair the damage done over the past decade to the Canadian Forces while reducing the national deficit. Then we will be ready again to loan combat ready forces and other resources to that elusive search for peace.

Major-General Lewis MacKenzie currently speaks in Canada, the United States and around the world. He is constantly looking for support in terms of training and equipment for all of the world's peacekeepers. Like all of the Master Negotiators I have interviewed, there is a strong link between these Master Negotiators' visions and the negotiating and influencing skills that are necessary to bring their visions to fruition. They aim high but are also realistic about what can and cannot be accomplished.

Develop and Use Concrete Examples

Let me preface this by saying that I grew up in a very frugal home. My children almost always have a snack before going to bed at night and their snack of choice is usually cereal. My son, in particular, had eyes that were bigger than his stomach. He would usually eat the first bowl of cereal, still think he was hungry, pour a second bowl of cereal, but eat very little of it.

Although we had talked about this many times (to the point that sometimes his psychologist Dad would even engage in nagging, knowing full well that this response on my part was totally ineffective), his wasting of cereal continued.

Then one night I had an inspiration. As usual, Andrew had had two bowls of cereal and had left quite a bit in the second bowl. His allowance at the time was five dollars a week. After we threw the remaining cereal in the garbage, I reached into my wallet and took out a five-dollar bill and let it drop into the garbage container. Andrew, who knows I am frugal, looked at me as if I had two heads.

In a very calm tone of voice, I told Andrew that each night he wasted cereal, it did not mean much, but over time it was like throwing money away. Andrew's eyes brightened as he looked up at me and said, "I get it Dad." By making the feedback salient and the example concrete, the message had been successfully delivered and received. After that night, very little cereal was wasted in our house.

Concrete examples can also help resolve very difficult value-laden disputes. One of the best examples is reported in Susskind and Field's *Dealing with an Angry Public*. This example takes place in the Greater Boston watershed. The people who managed the watershed became concerned because the deer population, which had no natural predators, was growing to the point where the deer actually threatened the sustainability of the forest by destroying all of the young trees. To make matters worse, the management of the watershed knew that within any given 100-year period, there was likely to be a tornado, hurricane or forest fire, and without the young saplings there was no way the forest could regenerate itself. Their solution was to have a controlled cull (killing) of 576 deer. As you can imagine, the protesters were out in full force the next day.

The watershed management wisely brought in a neutral mediator. At this point in time, the mediator decided that there was no way the parties could listen rationally to each other, as is often the case in value-laden conflicts. Instead, the mediator asked that several sections of the forest be fenced off with eight-foot high chain-link fence. In two-years' time the mediator asked both parties to meet at the fenced-off sites where they could see that the quality of the forest was radically different within the fenced-off areas, that is, there was new growth. Using this piece of salient feedback, all of the participants could see that they had a common problem. The mediator then asked both sides to brainstorm options that would ensure the sustainability of both the forest and the deer.

Have the Best BATNA

As explained in their best selling negotiating book, *Getting to Yes*, Fisher and Ury state that your BATNA (Best Alternative To a Negotiated Agreement) is your walk-away alternative. In other words, our BATNA is what we will do in the absence of a deal. For example, suppose your family was moving to Calgary and that you had fallen in love with and purchased a beautiful house in the Parkhill area, thinking it would be very easy to sell your gorgeous condo overlooking False Creek in Vancouver. Let us further assume that the

EXERCISE 2-1

Using Concrete Examples

Using the space below, describe a situation where concrete examples were used to help one party better understand the interests of another party.

_____

_____

_____

_____

_____

_____

_____

_____

Next, briefly describe a current situation you could make a stronger argument by using concrete examples.

_____

_____

_____

_____

_____

_____

_____

_____

From *The Seven Strategies of Master Negotiators* by Brad McRae © 2002, McGraw-Hill Ryerson.

bottom has dropped out of the real estate market in Vancouver, it is mid-November and that the housing market is 100 percent dead. You have only received one offer on your condo and that offer was substantially below market value.

Since it is not likely at this point that you will receive any other offers and you cannot afford to pay two mortgages, heat two homes and pay double insurance, it would at first seem as if you have no other choice but to accept the below-market-value on your condo and lose a significant amount of money. However, your BATNA is to rent the condo until the housing market improves. Since you live near the university, renting should prove relatively easy.

In negotiation, it is often advantageous to not only know your BATNA but to have a very good idea of the other side's BATNA. Let me give an example. Early in my career, I spent half my time building up my business in staff training and development and half my time employed as the regional coordinator for a national employee assistance program (EAP). After several years, my business had built to the point where I wanted to work full-time for myself. At the same time, the national EAP company that I worked for had acquired a local EAP company, making it necessary for me to put in a significant amount of overtime, which often is not compensated for in management positions. The company also wanted to make the regional coordinator position for the recently merged companies a full-time one, which I did not want.

The president of the company and I were in the process of negotiating compensation for the extra work that I had done as a prelude to my leaving the company. I asked the president what his BATNA was and he replied that it was the status quo, meaning that I would remain part-time and leave the position at a time of my choosing. I knew that this was unacceptable to him because he wanted to move forward with the merger of the two companies with a full-time regional coordinator as quickly as possible. At that point, I knew my objective of being fairly compensated for the extra work I had put in would be achieved, because I knew how much they wanted to fill my position with a full-time person.

Therefore, a major part of preparing for a negotiation—and a part that is often overlooked or not paid enough attention to—is identifying your BATNA, understanding the other side's BATNA, and doing a thorough comparison of the relative advantages and disadvantages of each.

Also remember that just because you have a good BATNA, or even if you have a weak BATNA, you must always look for opportunities to "Boost Your BATNA", that is, to make it better. One of the best ways to know how well-prepared you are regarding your BATNA and the other party's BATNA, is to fill in the Master Negotiator's Preparation Form (Figure 2-1)—rather than assume that you are well-prepared—and to update the form as you proceed through the negotiation.

Be Prepared, but Flexible

Gerald William's remarkable research (discussed in detail in Strategy 4, Understand Negotiating Styles) documented three of the qualities of Master Negotiators. Master Negotiators come to the table incredibly well-prepared, they are flexible and they have incredibly good self-control. It is the second quality, flexibility, to which we now turn our attention.

There are two mistakes we can make when it comes to flexibility. We can either be too flexible or not flexible enough.

THE VALUE OF BEING FLEXIBLE

In 1993 I approached Michelin Canada to see if I could sell them on the use of my course on negotiation and influencing skills. I had approached Michelin because I felt that would be a very interesting company to work with, as it was the largest private sector employer in the province of Nova Scotia. In addition, Michelin has earned a world-class reputation in making state-of-the-art tires, and is also renowned for having a very strong and progressive corporate culture. I called and set up a meeting with the head of their training department, Fred Bolivar.

After our discussions, Fred said that he thought the course would be a valuable addition to their training program. There was only one caveat.

Michelin did not use external trainers at the time. The reason for this was that Michelin was as particular about who influenced its corporate culture as it was about developing state-of-the-art tires. Fred, who is an innovative thinker and who always develops multiple options, suggested the following alternative: I could deliver a train-the-trainer course to one of Michelin's internal trainers so that Michelin could then give the course to Michelin employees and we could work out a royalty agreement for the use of my course.

My first inclination was to say no. After all, by that time I had spent seven years developing the course, and felt a strong sense of ownership over the course materials, exercises and case studies. If I said yes, I would be giving that material over to someone else. On the other hand, if I said no, Michelin Canada could easily find someone else to give the train-the-trainer course, and I would not only lose out on a short-term contract and royalty fees, but I would also lose out on the chance to learn about Michelin and its corporate culture. Thankfully I had the flexibility to say yes.

The results of that decision may surprise you; they certainly surprised me. Firstly, Fred discovered that the course was a complicated one and that it would take a great deal of time and effort to train one of Michelin's trainers to give the course. Secondly, my values and the values upon which the course is based were already very similar to Michelin's values. The result was that I would continue to teach the course whenever they needed it at Michelin Canada. Because of that decision, I have had the marvellous opportunity to work with one of the world's most successful and most innovative manufacturing companies. I also have had the opportunity to work with and learn from Fred, an extremely well-informed, knowledgeable and innovative professional in the area of staff training and development.

Fred was subsequently promoted to the position of corporate training manager at the Michelin North America headquarters in Greenville, South Carolina. As it turned out, Michelin North America wanted to provide a course on negotiation and influencing skills. In the end, I won the contract based on my eight years' experience with Michelin Canada and my ability to make the course content Michelin specific.

EXERCISE 2-2

Identifying the Benefits of Being Flexible

Think of a time where you were more flexible than you normally would be that resulted in unexpected positive benefits. Describe that situation in detail in the space provided below and the benefits that accrued to you from your ability to be flexible.

_____

_____

_____

_____

_____

What lessons can you derive from the above experience that will help you be more effective in the future?

_____

_____

_____

_____

_____

Conversely, think of times when being flexible worked against you. What did you learn from these situations?

_____

_____

_____

_____

_____

From *The Seven Strategies of Master Negotiators* by Brad McRae © 2002, McGraw-Hill Ryerson.

None of this would have happened if I had been too inflexible to consider doing a train-the-trainer course eight years ago.

Among the techniques that promote flexibility are: superb interviewing skills,[1] creative thinking, risk taking, asking high-yield questions, using diagnostic information-seeking skills,[2] and thinking outside the box. Exercise 2-2 has been designed for you to look more closely at situations where you were more flexible than you thought possible.

Expect the Unexpected

A number of years ago, I was working as a regional manager for a national company. The work was very demanding so I booked Thursday evenings as private time. During this time I took ice skating lessons with an extremely capable coach. My friend and colleague, Harold Taylor, a nationally recognized expert on time management, taught me that if I wanted to protect my private time, I had to schedule it into my daily planner and second, that I had to treat it as equally important to other meetings that I had. He also warned me that I would be tested. I started my lessons, was making progress, and was feeling that I was getting a complete break from my work. In other words, I was feeling very good about taking care of myself. Little did I realize that I would be tested so soon, or so often.

The following Thursday, the president and CEO of the national organization was paying a site visit in Halifax and a business dinner was scheduled for that night. I asked if we could eat early because I had a meeting Thursday night (I did—although it was with my coach). The next week, the vice-president was in town and once again we had a business dinner scheduled for Thursday night. Again, I asked if we could eat early because I had a meeting scheduled for later that evening—with my coach. I was beginning to feel like I had mastered one of the elements of time management and self-care.

The next Thursday I was thoroughly tested. My children attend École Beaufort, which is the French immersion school in our neighbourhood. Thursday night was the school's celebration of La Carnival, which recognizes the coming of spring. My son Andrew very much wanted the whole family to go to La Carnival. I thought that this was a teachable moment where I could help my son learn that parents deserved some private time as well. I carefully prepared for this negotiation. I was going to talk about the fact that I take my son to hockey and soccer on a regular basis, that we had a father and son trip once a year, played sports together, etc. However, before I made these points, as a good negotiator does, I asked my son "Why is it so important to you that I go to La Carnival?" This gorgeous blond, blue-eyed eight-year-old looked up at me and said, "Dad, because I like you a lot."

I was wiped off the table. Speechless. I thought about it all the next day and came up with the following interest-based solution. My main interest was taking the lesson and for one night could easily miss the warm-up and cool-down. So I approached Andrew and asked him if it would be all right if we went as a family to the start of La Carnival. I would take my lesson, but miss the warm-up and cool-down and be back at the school by eight o'clock. "Sure Dad." By taking an interest-based approach, both parties' interests were well satisfied.

There are several important lessons for all Master Negotiators in this story. Firstly, you must always expect the unexpected. Secondly, if you cannot see an immediate solution, take a break from the table. Thirdly, by focusing on interests rather than immediate solutions, a creative solution can be found so that all of the parties' interests can be well satisfied.

Use Role Play

As has already been stated, one of the biggest mistakes you can make as a negotiator is to enter your negotiations overly confident and under prepared. One of the best ways to avoid this mistake is to role-play the negotiation. Let me first give two examples of how this technique paid off for two of my clients.

LASMO Nova Scotia[3] was a petroleum exploration company. They found oil off Sable Island, Nova Scotia, and formed a partnership with the Government of Nova Scotia by partnering with a crown corporation, Nova Scotia Resources Ltd. (NSRL).

LASMO, under the leadership of the vice-president of finance and adminis-tration, was preparing for a meeting with NSRL regarding cost sharing related to the maintenance of the drilling platform. The vice-president and the LASMO team thought they were very well-prepared to enter negotiations. I suggested that it would be a good idea to be absolutely sure that they were well pre-pared. One of the best ways to verify their level of preparation was to role-play the opening round of the negotiation, with half the LASMO staff playing them-selves and the other half playing the role of their counterparts at NSRL.

An hour into the role play, the vice-president wisely called a halt to the exercise. He and everyone else had determined that they were not as well-pre-pared as they wanted to be, and that some of their reasoning was not as strong as it could have been. He credits the role play with saving LASMO from making a costly mistake.

I also had the opportunity to work with staff from both the Grace Maternity Hospital and the Isaac Walton Killam (IWK) Children's Hospital in Halifax prior to the merging of the two hospitals into the IWK-Grace Health Centre. Naturally, there was a great deal of uncertainty, anxiety and fear among the employees. There would be some job losses and new department heads would need to be selected. When emotions are running high, we all tend to become stressed, to think in terms of simple stereotypes, and we are less likely to develop creative solutions.

I had previously taught my course on negotiation and influencing skills to all of the middle and senior management at the Grace. When the merger into shared services was announced, I was working with the IWK side and suggested that they role-play a crucial meeting regarding the integration of the services. The IWK staff reported that they had obtained a much deeper insight into the interests of the Grace Maternity Hospital's departments and would therefore be able to negotiate in a much more open manner based upon what they had come to realize were the true interests of the Grace's depart-ments, rather than based on the stereotypes they had of their counterparts.

If you are entering a difficult and/or important negotiation, it can be equally helpful for you to find someone who would role-play with you.

Explain the situation as carefully as possible to the person, or persons, with whom you are doing the role play. Then play your role while the other person plays the role of the person with whom you will negotiate. There are many lessons that can be learned from this exercise. Firstly, you will get to hear how your arguments sound, secondly, you will be afforded the opportunity to react to "your words" from the vantage point of the other party, and thirdly, you can take advantage of the adage that "you can't change someone's mind if you don't know where their mind is." In other words, you can have a dress rehearsal to further develop your logic, increase your understanding of the other party's interests and bring additional options to the table. All of this will increase the likelihood of creating optimal rather than sub-optimal solutions.

Use Objective Criteria

Disraeli said: "As a general rule, the most successful people in the world are those who have the best information." Many difficult negotiations can be made much easier through the judicious use of objective criteria. Using objective criteria, I mean using obtained objective empirical evidence, can help all of the parties make better decisions in not only the negotiation, but in developing a more effective negotiation *process*. Three advantages of using objective criteria are:

1. it helps the participants step back and take a more objective look at their concerns;
2. it adds a new perspective or way of looking at a problem; and
3. it helps the parties save face as they move from their original positions to a new solution.

I would like to demonstrate the power of using objective criteria in an example concerning safety during public skating.

For a long time, I have been concerned with the lack of safety standards during public skating. My children and I skate a great deal at various rinks in our city, and only one of the rinks took the matter of safety during public skating seriously. I had three main concerns: firstly, the doors to the rink were often left open which increased the possibility of head injury, secondly, skaters often sat on the boards, and thirdly, skaters often climbed over the boards to get onto the ice, both of which meant that serious injuries could result if another skater fell into their skates.

I brought these matters to the attention of the facilities manager for our city and asked him what the city's policy was on safety during public skating. He told me that the city had no written policy. In fact, Vancouver Parks and Recreation had developed the only Canadian policy I could find and it was not very specific.

I then contacted Dr. Brent Taylor, the head of emergency services at the IWK Children's Hospital. He told me that keeping the doors open during public skating increased both the frequency and severity of head injuries. Lastly, I contacted The Canadian Hospitals Injury Reporting and Prevention Program (CHIRPP). CHIRPP has a database of all injuries that are reported and seen in emergency rooms at all of the pediatric hospitals and at six general hospitals across Canada.

CHIRPP completed a search of all of the injuries that took place in ice rinks during the times when hockey was not being played and the findings supported my concerns about the need for safety standards at public ice rinks. Once I presented all of this data to the Halifax Regional Municipality (HRM), the city's officials developed a comprehensive policy designed to prevent needless injuries during public skating. The HRM now has the most progressive policy on ice rink safety of any Canadian municipality. As a result, Halifax will have fewer preventable accidents. Our insurance rates will also decrease because the attendants, whose responsibility it is to enforce this policy, have been better trained. None of this would have occurred without the use of objective information in supporting my arguments. To paraphrase one of Teddy Roosevelt's most famous sayings, "Always speak softly and carry a large statistic."

EXERCISE 2-3

Using Objective Criteria

In the space below think of an example where objective criteria was used to help negotiations be more effective and persuasive.

_____

_____

_____

_____

_____

_____

_____

_____

Next, briefly describe a current situation where you could make a stronger argument by using objective criteria.

_____

_____

_____

_____

_____

_____

From *The Seven Strategies of Master Negotiators* by Brad McRae © 2002, McGraw-Hill Ryerson.

Determine Your Leverage

Leverage can be defined as the relative advantage one party has over the other at the bargaining table. Master Negotiators always examine those factors that would contribute and those that would take away from each side's leverage before sitting down at the bargaining table. The five factors are:

1. Who needs the deal the most?
2. Who is under the most pressure to complete the deal?
3. Who has the tightest timeline and/or deadline?
4. Who values the relationship the most?
5. Who has the strongest BATNA?

For example, if you have to buy a new car because "Old Betsey" just died, you are in a weaker bargaining position relative to the person selling you a new car. If on the other hand, you start looking for a car well in advance; have compared the relative advantages of buying new, buying used or leasing; have determined the dealer cost of the car if you decide to buy a new car; have bids from three or more car dealers; and know that it is the end of the month and recent car sales have been poor, then you have the relative advantage.

Write Down Possible Trade Offs

There are three reasons Master Negotiators write down their own and the other party's possible trade offs or concessions. The first is so you can determine the concessions' true cost or value to you when you are not under the pressure of negotiating at the table. The second reason is that by writing down and prioritizing your trade offs you will guard against the tendency of either giving away too much (once you have put a trade off or concession on the table it is difficult to remove it) or too little. If too little, the other party may lose interest in the negotiation and pursue their goals elsewhere. The third advantage of listing your trade offs or concessions and those of the other party is so you can ask for your colleagues' input and suggestions. The results are often more creative negotiations for all parties.

FIGURE 2-1

The Master Negotiator's Preparation Form

Interests	
Our Interests	**Their Interests**

The Prize: The Ultimate Outcome from the Negotiation	
Our Prize	**Their Prize**

From *The Seven Strategies of Master Negotiators* by Brad McRae © 2002, McGraw-Hill Ryerson.

FIGURE 2-1 . . . *Continued*

The Master Negotiator's Preparation Form

Options	
Our Options	**Their Options**

Standards
(Objective standards or objective criteria help the parties look at the negotiation much more objectively and make it easier to reach an agreement)

Offers
Aspire to? (The best arrangement you could get)
Content with? (Satisfactory)
Live with? (Acceptable minimal settlement)

BATNA (Best Alternative To a Negotiated Agreement)	
Our BATNA	**Their BATNA**

From *The Seven Strategies of Master Negotiators* by Brad McRae © 2002, McGraw-Hill Ryerson.

FIGURE 2-1 . . . *Continued*

The Master Negotiator's Preparation Form

Leverage	
Our Leverage	**Their Leverage**

Possible Trade Offs/Concessions	
Our Trade Offs/Concessions	**Their Trade Offs/Concessions**

From *The Seven Strategies of Master Negotiators* by Brad McRae © 2002, McGraw-Hill Ryerson.

Our Opening Statement

In summary, the 10 guidelines reviewed in this Strategy will help you come to the negotiating table incredibly well-prepared whereas your more amateur counterparts may come to the table overly confident and under prepared. One of the best ways to circumvent the natural tendency to assume that we are well-prepared—and finding out too late that we are not—is to fill out the Master Negotiators' Preparation Form, reproduced in Figure 2-1.[4]

---

[1] These skills will be defined in greater detail at a later point in this book.

[2] These skills will be defined in greater detail at a later point in this book.

[3] LASMO Nova Scotia was sold to Pan Canadian in January, 1996.

[4] Other terms that are used with the form will be explained throughout the book, and additional copies of the form can be downloaded from the What's New page at **www.bradmcrae.com.**

STRATEGY 3

Create and Claim Maximum Value

Cooperative negotiators do a great job at creating value; competitive negotiators do a great job at claiming value; Master Negotiators are experts at doing both.

— *Brad McRae*

Creating value and claiming value are at the heart of the negotiation process. Creating value is our ability to effectively develop creative solutions to best meet all the needs and interests of all parties at the negotiating table. This process is commonly known as expanding the pie. Claiming value is our ability to effectively get our needs and interests met through the negotiating process. Claiming value refers to how much of the pie we receive as a result of the negotiation process.

Most negotiators do a good job either at creating value or at claiming value. Master Negotiators do a good job of both. In fact, it is the judicious juxtaposition of these two skill sets that determine how well we negotiate, as the following example points out.

In 1991, the Soviet Union was disintegrating. Suddenly, to everyone's surprise, there were now a number of new countries in Eastern Europe, all of which wanted a Canadian embassy. Canada was in a recession at the time, so there was no money to be spent on new embassies. The first step in approaching these negotiations would be to develop a list of each side's interests and prioritizing those interests. For example, the prioritized list of interests for Canada and for the new countries might look something like the list presented in Figure 3-1.

Of course there may be many more than four interests; the Law of Four is a rule of thumb that was designed to make sure that the most salient interests have been noted. In rare cases there may be less than four. However, Master Negotiators have determined that the better job one does at identifying and prioritizing the interests of both parties, the more likely it is that a creative solution will be found.

After the interests have been determined, verified and prioritized, it is time to develop creative options that will best meet the needs of all of the

FIGURE 3-1

Identifying Interests

Canada's Interests	The New Countries' Interests
Increase trade with the new countries	To be recognized by the world community including Canada
Represent Canadian citizens' interests in the new countries	Increase trade with Canada
Represent the needs, wants and aspirations of the diverse ethnic groups that reside in Canada	To receive foreign aid from Canada.
Be a good global citizen	To increase the number of Canadian tourists who visit.

parties. Using the Law of Four, we develop at least four options. Possible options are presented in Figure 3-2.

FIGURE 3-2

Identifying Options

1. Not building any embassies.
2. Establishing a few embassies in centralized areas to serve all of the countries.
3. Establishing consulates in each of the countries.
4. Share embassy space with another country.

In the end, the best solution was for Canada and Australia to share embassy space. Both countries are of a similar size and population and have similar political outlooks. Both Canada and Australia only had to pay half of the cost of each embassy, and the host countries gained international recognition.

Now, let's imagine that in Tallinn, the capital of Estonia, both Canada and Australia decide to share a beautiful historic four-storey brownstone building. On the fourth floor there is one very large spacious office with plate glass windows that give a gorgeous view of the city and the Gulf of Finland. Also on the fourth floor are two not nearly so nicely appointed medium sized offices. Claiming value could be whose ambassador, Canada's or Australia's, gets the most prestigious office. Of course, the most creative solution would be to use the large office as a boardroom. When the Canadian Ambassador needed to use the boardroom, the Canadian flag would be brought in, and when the Australian Ambassador needed to use the boardroom, the Australian flag would be brought in and the two ambassadors would each have the use of the medium sized offices.

There are seven steps Master Negotiators use to create and claim maximum value:

1. Identify your own and the other party's interests.
2. Search for and identify common ground.
3. Agree on a procedure for data collection.
4. Develop creative options.
5. Take a break from the table and solicit creative solutions from other people who are not actively involved in the negotiation.
6. Do a pros and cons analysis, then maximize all of the pros.
7. Develop a culture that recognizes and rewards innovative creative solutions.

Among the skills that Master Negotiators use to create value are identifying the interests of both parties and then developing creative options to expand the pie. Among the skills that are necessary to expand the pie are active listening, identifying interests, linking interests and developing options (brainstorming) to satisfy interests and arrive at optimal solutions.

Claiming value is defined as how well our interests are met or satisfied during a negotiation. Among the skills that are necessary to claim value are coming to the table incredibly well-prepared, having a good BATNA (Best Alternative To a Negotiated Agreement), being articulate, persuasive and assertive about our interests, having excellent presentation and diplomatic skills, and being influential. Claiming value can also include dirty tricks and pressure tactics; becoming aggressive; using intimidation, threats and violence; and misleading, lying and advantageously shaping the opponents' perception of the bargaining range.

The concepts of creating and claiming value are a lot like adding just the right amount of salt to the soup. Master chefs have had so much experience that they easily add the right amount. Master Negotiators have had so much experience and practice with the concepts of creating and claiming value that the skills become second nature. Until the rest of us reach that level, we will need to work on developing these two critical skills and develop procedures for us to get salient feedback as to which skills we perform well and which we need to work on.

There are two easy ways to get feedback on how well you create value. The first is simply to rate yourself from one to 10 on your ability to create value on one of your last negotiations. Then do the same thing on your ability to claim value on that same negotiation. If you do this three times, either on past negotiations or on on-going negotiation you will probably see a pattern that indicates that you are better at one or the other of these processes. Please note that it is a good idea to rate yourself on either negotiations at work or at home. I recommend that you do not mix your sample because you may negotiate very differently in these two settings. Lastly, you should also know that Master Negotiators rate themselves on creating and claiming value *during* the negotiation process as well as after. Rating yourself during the process allows time for strategies and mid-course corrections based on the feedback received from your ratings. Exercise 3-1 has been designed to help develop these essential skills.

In addition to being an expert at preparation for negotiations, **Frank King** is an expert at creating and claiming value, as the following story so aptly illustrates. Frank King was the driving force in Calgary, Alberta's successful bid to host the XVth Winter Olympics in 1988. His vision for the Calgary Winter Olympics was to put on the best Winter Olympics to date. He also very much wanted the Games to leave a legacy for future generations in the world-class sports facilities that would be built in Calgary. In fact, in place of the usual deficit after the Games, the Calgary Winter Olympics left an operating profit of $46 million, and this money was used to finance sports activities in Calgary and across the country. In recognition of this achievement, Frank was inducted into the Order of Canada in 1988.

During Frank's eight years as chair of Calgary's Olympic Organizing Committee, he conducted thousands of negotiations. He had 485 staff, 9,400 volunteers, and oversaw the construction of $350 million in sports facilities.

When I interviewed Frank King from his home in Calgary, Alberta, I was impressed right from the start by the friendliness and energy in his voice. After the introductions and the explanation of the purpose of my call and upon getting Frank's agreement to participate in this project, I asked him

EXERCISE 3-1

Creating and Claiming Value Evaluation Form

In the following questions, a 1 indicates that you created little or no value and a 10 indicates that you created a great deal of value.

	Created little or no value					Created a great deal of value			

1. In your last negotiation at home or at work, how well did you create value?

   1 2 3 4 5 6 7 8 9 10

2. In the same negotiation, how well did you claim value?

   1 2 3 4 5 6 7 8 9 10

3. (a) In the next three negotiations you enter, rate your effectiveness in creating value.

   First negotiation   1 2 3 4 5 6 7 8 9 10

   Second negotiation   1 2 3 4 5 6 7 8 9 10

   Third negotiation   1 2 3 4 5 6 7 8 9 10

   (b) Now, rate your effectiveness in claiming value for these same three negotiations.

   First negotiation   1 2 3 4 5 6 7 8 9 10

   Second negotiation   1 2 3 4 5 6 7 8 9 10

   Third negotiation   1 2 3 4 5 6 7 8 9 10

4. Examine the above pattern. What three recommendations can you make to yourself to improve your ability to create and claim value?

   1. _____

   _____

   2. _____

   _____

   3. _____

   _____

when a good time would be for a 15- to 20-minute interview. His response was that now was as good a time as any. I knew then and there that I was dealing with a decisive, goal-oriented individual.

During our interview, we spoke about two of Frank's most important negotiations: the negotiations with the International Olympic Committee (IOC) in the bid to bring the Games to Calgary, and the negotiation for the American television rights. In reading the interview, please note how Frank thoroughly identifies the interests of each party and then develops creative solutions to maximize each and every interest and how he demonstrates his expertise at creating and claiming maximum value.

B.M. *How did you prepare for the Calgary bid for the Games?*

F.K. It was essential to obtain and verify our understanding of the other parties' point of view even though the tendency is to focus on what we wanted to get. The way we approached the whole Olympic project was to understand what it is like to be an IOC member, what they are looking for and how they choose a host site. Therefore, one of the first things we did was to develop as comprehensive a profile as possible of what they wanted. We then enriched the profile by asking them as specifically as possible what their criteria was in selecting a city to host the Games, and it was through this interactive process that our profile of what they wanted became more and more accurate. This is important because most cities approached the Games to enrich the city itself. We placed our efforts on enriching the Games first, and the city second. In other words, they were the client/customer, and our job was to satisfy the customer's needs better than anyone else.

> *It was essential to obtain and verify our understanding of the other parties' point of view even though the tendency is to focus on what we wanted to get.*
>
> **Frank King**

Secondly, we were very systematic. We looked at what we could offer and what we could not, and then looked to develop creative options. We developed a very specific checklist of what they wanted and what we could offer. We made sure that what they wanted was on our list, and then went over and over the checklist to make sure that there wasn't anything missing. We treated it as a job interview. They were hiring us to run the Games. We had to earn their trust.

Because of our preparation, we were tuned in more precisely to what the Olympic movement was about and more specifically what the IOC wanted for the Winter Games. After the Games, many people asked for my help in getting the Games for their city. They wanted to improve the quality of their city, get an economic boost and create world-class training venues. But more than anyone else, we concentrated on what we could do for the Olympic movement and more specifically for the Winter Games.

B.M. *Could you give me a second example of creating and claiming value?*

F.K. We used the same approach when negotiating with all of the television networks. The network executives that we negotiated with said every previous organizing city had asked what the television networks needed, but they had never gotten it. We proved to them we would be different. By listening very carefully to their needs and again using our checklist system to make sure that we did what we said we would do, we won their trust.

More specifically, the television networks' four most basic needs were to increase viewership, to increase revenue, to have the most popular events scheduled during prime viewing time, and to have the best TV camera locations and viewing angles possible. We delivered on all four.

To deliver on our promises, we first changed the number of days of the Games from 10 to 16. This was crucial because at 10 days, there is only one weekend and the weekend is when the television networks secured their highest ratings and hence their highest revenue. When we changed the Winter Games to 16 days, we were able to provide two weekends of higher ratings and higher revenue for the television networks. As a result we got the first major television contract for the Winter Games. Eight years previously, the Lake Placid Winter Games received $30 million for the American TV rights. In Calgary, we received over $300 million for the American contract, which went a long way in helping to make our Games profitable.

The Calgary Winter Games were a huge success for the city of Calgary, for the Canadian athletes and for the athletes from all of the 57 countries who competed. It was a success for the viewing public who attended the Games and watched the Games on television, and a success for the television network. In large measure the Games were a success because Frank King knew the importance of preparation, thoroughly identifying the parties' interests, developing options and creating and claiming value.

We will now look at the seven steps Master Negotiators use to create and claim value.

Step 1: Identify Interests

We have seen how the Law of Four was applied to identify Canada's interests and the new countries of Eastern Europe, and how Frank King so aptly identified the interests of the ICO and the television networks in making the Calgary Winter Olympics as successful as they were. Unfortunately one of the biggest mistakes negotiators make is to assume that they have done a good enough job at identifying their own and the other party's interests when in fact they have not adequately done so. The Master Negotiators' Preparation Form (Figure 2-1) will let us see clearly whether or not we have adequately identified all of the parties' interests. Identifying all of the parties' interests is integral to the process of creating and claiming value, which is at the heart of all negotiations.

Step 2: Search for and Identify Common Ground

There are four techniques that make it much more likely that the parties will focus on common ground: develop incredibly good framing statements, keep your eye on the prize, examine each party's Worst Alternative To a Negotiated Agreement (WATNA), and examine failed negotiations.

DEVELOP EXCELLENT FRAMING STATEMENTS

Ninety percent of the way a negotiation finishes depends on the way that it starts. Developing a good framing statement helps the participants begin to focus on creative integrative solutions that will best meet the needs and interests of all of the parties.

An excellent framing statement is critical to the success of stage one negotiation (when the parties first decide that they have enough in common to come to the table and begin the negotiation process). Since 90 percent of the way a negotiation ends is dependent on how it begins, we must pay careful attention to this important stage. The framing statement answers the question as to why the parties have entered negotiations and what they hope to achieve from the process. The framing statement is as inclusive and neutral as possible in representing all of the parties' overriding interests. For example, the framing statement for a couple going to marriage counselling is:

> Not to save the couple's marriage, but to help the couple make the wisest decision possible as to what they want to do with their marriage.

An example of a framing statement for a couple in the process of separating and divorcing is:

> We are here today to see if we can develop options that will help you
> maximize your assets and minimize the costs associated with your
> divorce. At the same time, we will work on developing a shared par-
> enting agreement that is fair and equitable to both the parents and
> to the children.

A third example of a framing statement is one that was developed when a
controversy arose between Mothers Against Drunk Driving (MADD) and the
Department of Transportation and Public Works over the safety of MADD's
white cross program. The program involved holding road-side commemorative
services and placing white crosses and wreaths by the side of the road where
fatalities had occurred due to drunk driving. The program served as both a
reminder of the tragic consequences of and as a deterrent to driving while
intoxicated. The Department of Transportation and Public Works was concerned that the road-side program could unfortunately contribute to driver
inattention, the cause of one-third of all automobile accidents. The framing
statement that they used to identify common ground at the start of their
meetings was:

> We are here today to see if we can develop options that will help
> MADD to alert the general public as to the dire consequences of
> drunk drivers and at the same time helping the relatives feel that
> their loved ones did not die in vain by commemorating the sites of
> the accidents. At the same time, the safety of the general public must
> not be put at risk by having markers that would distract the public
> from their driving and thus increase the likelihood of an accident.

KEEP YOUR EYE ON THE PRIZE

One of the best pieces of advice from William Ury's highly acclaimed book,
Getting Past No, is to keep your eye on the prize. Keeping your eye on the
prize means keeping your eye on the "ultimate outcome you want from
the negotiation at the deepest level possible." For example, if you

are negotiating with one of only two suppliers for a particular product you need in order to run your business, allowing yourself to get too angry and "fire" one of the suppliers may feel good for 15 seconds, however, at the end of those 15 seconds you have made your business hostage to your one and only remaining supplier.

One of the best examples of keeping your eye on the prize in a business setting has to do with the merger of two companies. Mergers are inherently difficult as there are almost always winners and losers and there is the inevitable clash between the two distinct organizational cultures. It is also true that most organizations do not pay enough attention to the process by which the merger takes place. This is important because the process by which the merger takes place is the foundation upon which the new merged organization will be built on, as the following example illustrates. The example is taken from Norman R. Augustine, CEO of Lockheed Martin, in his insightful article, entitled "Reshaping an industry: Lockheed Martin's survival story."[1] In the article, Augustine chronicles how the U.S. defence industry decreased procurement by more than 60 percent since 1989 as a result of the end of the Cold War. Consequently, 15 major companies were downsized and merged into four. Augustine stated that when Lockheed and Martin Marietta were merged, they had two headquarters buildings, but only needed one. They selected the building that would be most appropriate for the new combined organization. Next they selected the best people from both organizations to lead the new one. Then Augustine did something that was critical to the success of the new organization. He moved all of the employees out of what was previously the head office of one of the companies that were merged, and he then moved the new team in. Therefore, both figuratively and literally, they were off to a new and fair start.

Was the cost of moving everyone out and then moving some of those same people back in worth the cost? You bet. Augustine had his eye on the prize, a new company with a fresh start, with all employees feeling that they were treated as fairly as possible.

EXAMINE EACH PARTY'S WATNA (WORST ALTERNATIVE TO A NETOGIATED AGREEMENT)

The parties can help avoid sub-optimal outcomes by addressing their WATNAs at the outset of the negotiation. One example of a WATNA is the divorcing couple that spends all of its time in court trying to best each other as to who will get the most assets. However, at the end, neither party has anything left because all of their remaining resources are tied up in legal fees. A similar example from the business world is two competitive companies that spend all of their resources battling each other, devoting nothing to research and development, only to find that a young new company has built a better product and as such has garnered most if not all of the market share.

EXAMINE FAILED NEGOTIATIONS

Examining failed negotiations can be done by looking at our personal negotiations that failed, by asking for an outside expert opinion on a personal negotiation that failed and by examining others' examples of failed negotiations. The most frequently identified cause for failure is not finding enough common ground. (See the discussion in Strategy 4 on Hydro-Québec and the Cree negotiations for an excellent example of the failure to find common ground.)

Step 3: Agree on a Procedure for Data Collection

Instead of being adversarial, agree on a procedure of how to collect data so that the parties can make the wisest decision possible. In the example from Strategy 2, where the Department of Recreation of the Halifax Regional Municipality and I disagreed on the issue of safety during public skating at the city's ice rinks, I presented evidence on the number of accidents from the Canadian Hospitals Injury Reporting and Prevention Program. An alternative would be for the parties to jointly agree in advance on a procedure for data collection. Having the parties agree ahead of time can make the process less adversarial.

Step 4: Develop Creative Options

If not adequately identifying each of the party's interests is the first mistake that negotiators make, then not identifying enough options is the second. By fully understanding each party's interests and by developing at least four options, you are much more likely to develop creative rather than wasteful solutions. The following provides a perfect example.

During the 1990s, cost cutting measures were put into place in most major firms, as the business world became increasingly competitive. One solution to this dilemma was outsourcing. That is, functions that could be more economically done outside of an organization such as printing, human resources and payroll were outsourced to another firm at considerable cost-savings to the host organization.

Maritime Medical Care[2] had an excellent printing department, however, it was not in full use all of the time. Therefore one option was to keep the status quo. The advantage of this option was that employee morale would not suffer, but a potential cost savings would not be realized. A second option would be to look for efficiencies in how the printing department was run, and a third option was to outsource printing. The fourth option was to let the printing department compete for printing contracts in the open market. All of the profits from any external work would be divided 60 percent for Maritime Medical Care to cover the operating and maintenance costs of using Maritime Medical Care's equipment, and 40 percent would be divided up among the employees of the printing department on a fair and equitable basis. In other words, the employees from the printing department would become intrepreneurs (entrepreneurs working within an existing company as opposed to starting up and running their own company).

The first year, the manager of the printing department at Maritime Medical Care added $10,000 to his paycheque. Other employees in the printing department did equally as well. Maritime Medical Care was now in a position where the printing department went from being a cost centre to a profit centre. Employee morale in the department went through the roof. Jim Moir, president and CEO of Maritime Medical Care, and his management team also developed a precedent that other departments could consider, so not only was this a very creative solution to this particular problem, it was also a mental model that other employees and departments could use to help them develop more creative solutions to the problems that they currently faced and would face in the future.

Master Negotiators put twice as many options on the table by using the Law of Four and "going wide before going deep." The Law of Four means that we explore at least four options. Going wide before going deep means that we must consider all of our options before considering any one of them in detail. The reason for this is that if we start exploring one of the various options first, it makes it 100 times more likely that we will overlook options that could lead to more creative solutions. The Law of Four and going wide before going deep, force us to think and act more like Master Negotiators. The more we think and act like successful negotiators, the greater the probability that we will *become* successful negotiators.

Step 5: Take a Break from the Table

Almost everyone has had the experience of working on a difficult problem or of being in a difficult negotiation when something—a telephone call, a colleague at the door, a washroom trip—forces you to take a spontaneous break from the problem or negotiation. Then suddenly, when you are not consciously thinking about the problem, you get an insight that leads to a solution.

Master Negotiators know inherently when it is time to take a break from the problem or negotiation to give themselves time for their subconscious to work on it or to give them the perspective necessary to develop a creative solution.

Master Negotiators also know when it is time to get outside help. No matter how creative we are there will be times when we just cannot see an outside-the-box solution. Master Negotiators will take advantage of their ability to network with the right people at the right time to find that elusive creative solution. This point is extremely well documented in Daniel Goleman's bestseller *Emotional Intelligence*.

In the book, Goleman cites a superb example of the power of networking in generating creative solutions. Goleman describes a study that was undertaken at Bell Labs in Princeton, New Jersey. Bell Labs is a think tank, which employs engineers and scientists most of whom are geniuses with IQs over 140. The dependent variable in this study, that is, what was being measured, was the productivity of these engineers and scientists as measured by the number of products they developed and the number of patents they secured. The study measured the scientists' and engineers' ability to network by obtaining permission to read their e-mails. What this study found was that productivity was not related to IQ, but to EQ (emotional intelligence). The most productive scientists and engineers, when faced with a problem, would e-mail colleagues throughout the world. Within a very short period of time, they received responses that contained the answer, a partial answer or a process whereby the scientist or engineer could develop the answer to the problem and hence develop another product or patent. The scientists and engineers who had less well-developed networks—no matter what their IQ— were rated as significantly less productive.

I would like to offer the reader a personal example of the power of networking. I was in the process of preparing a course in which I wanted to use an intriguing case study I called "Our Town vs. the Asphalt Company." Two groups would be working on the case simultaneously. I wanted to use video-taped feedback, which is one of the best ways for the participants to see what they did right as well as to note targets for improvement. The problem was that I did not have the time to record both sections and then go over the tapes to pick the salient points to play back to the groups.

I called a colleague, Fay Cohen, in the Department of Environmental Studies at Dalhousie University and asked for her advice. Fay suggested that I play the role of a local TV reporter. In that role I would only videotape the negotiations at set critical times: each participant would be privately video-taped after reading his or her role but before entering into the negotiations and during the transition from one stage to the next for his or her reaction to the other negotiators and to the progress or lack thereof. Then, when the negotiations were complete, I videotaped each team's joint communiqué to the press. The result was that the participants could see how the positions and interests of all of the parties changed during the course of the consensus building exercise in a process that was very similar to watching time-lapse photography, and each person received extremely valuable feedback on their negotiating style.

All it took was one simple phone call and a five-minute conversation with the right person at the right time. This is why all Master Negotiators have a network of people they can call upon. I once came upon a formula that stated that our Effectiveness equals our Abilities times our Relationships ($E = A \times R$). These two examples of networking attest to the power of developing, enhancing and using one's networking skills to negotiate and solve problems more effectively.

Step 6: Do a Pros and Cons Analysis, then Maximize the Pros

Making a list of all of the pros and cons of various options and then combining all of the pros and brainstorming a solution that satisfies all of the pros is a technique that is guaranteed to stretch your thinking and that of those around you. At the same time this technique ensures that you have developed the most robust solution possible and that gains are not left on the table. The best way to illustrate this technique is with an example. This case study centres on the merger of two fictitious companies but in actual fact was based on a real event. The names of the two fictitious companies are Networking Solutions of Toronto and Internet Connections of Ottawa.

The goal of this case study is to decide on a unified human resource policy that will satisfy the needs of all of the employees from the two companies that were merged to become Networking Connections. I will first present the case study, and then the list of the pros and cons for the two solutions that were placed on the table, followed by a robust solution based solely on the pros from each of the previous proposals.

CASE STUDY: NETWORKING SOLUTIONS VS. INTERNET CONNECTIONS[3]

Confidential Instructions for Internet Connections of Ottawa:

Intranet software is specialized software that allows an organization to establish a secure private internetwork within their company. During the past six years, Internet Connections of Ottawa and Networking Solutions of Toronto each developed state-of-the-art intranet software. Both companies became fierce competitors both domestically and internationally.

Two years ago, one of North America's largest automobile manufacturers sent out a request for proposal to develop intranet software. Both Internet Connections and Networking Solutions bid on the project not thinking they had a chance of securing the contract, but they wanted the experience of bidding on such an important international contract.

Several months later, both Internet Connections and Networking Solutions were stunned to learn that they would be awarded the contract due to their superior Canadian technology, but only if they agreed to work jointly on the project.

Due to the magnitude of the project, the only sensible thing to do was to merge the two companies into one. It was agreed that the name of the new company would be Networking Connections. Each of the organizations selected three of their top employees to head the transition team. Both companies were about the same size, but had two very distinct organizational cultures.

All of the issues regarding the merger of the company were worked out reasonably well with one exception. It seemed like such a small problem that it was left until last. However, even after working on this issue for two days, no acceptable solution was developed that would meet the needs of the employees in both the Ottawa and the Toronto locations. A description of the problem is as follows.

Internet Connections was well known for its progressive human resource policies, which made it one of the best IT firms to work for in the Ottawa region. Internet Connections had both flexible working hours and flex-time. The difference between flexible working hours and flex-time is as follows.

Flexible working hours means that employees can, with the consent of their department, choose which seven and one-half hours they work per day. For example, if it met the needs of the department the employee could start work at 7:00 A.M. and stop at 3:30 P.M. or start at 10:00 A.M. and stop at 6:30 P.M. The employee could also vary the start and stop time to meet their individual needs, as long as the needs of the department and the organization as a whole were well met.

Flex-time on the other hand meant that an employee could work fewer than seven and one-half hours one day and make up the time on another day. It also meant that employees could work longer hours and could bank as much as one week's hours (37.5) and take that time as holiday time as long as the needs of the department and the organization were satisfied. There was no way that the employees of the former Internet Connections in Ottawa were going to give this up. A line has to be drawn in the sand and it is time to take a stand!

The president has decreed that there has to be one uniform policy for the new merged company. The transition team has 30 minutes to come up with options to solve this dilemma before presenting its solution to the new president and CEO of Networking Connections.

Confidential Instructions for Networking Solutions of Toronto:
Intranet software is specialized software that allows an organization to establish a secure private internetwork within their company. During the past six years, Networking Solutions of Toronto and Internet Connections of Ottawa each developed state-of-the-art intranet software. Both companies became fierce competitors both domestically and internationally.

Two years ago, one of North America's largest automobile manufacturers sent out a request for proposal to develop intranet software. Both Networking Solutions and Internet Connections bid on the project not thinking they had a chance of securing the contract, but they wanted the experience of bidding on such an important international contract.

Several months later, both Networking Solutions and Internet Connections were stunned to learn that they would be awarded the contract due to their superior Canadian technology, but only if they agreed to work jointly on the project.

Due to the magnitude of the project, the only sensible thing to do was to merge the two companies into one. It was agreed that the name of the new company would be Networking Connections. Each of the organizations selected three of their top employees to head the transition team. Both companies were about the same size, but had two very distinct organizational cultures.

All of the issues regarding the merger of the company were worked out reasonably well with one exception. It seemed like such a small problem that it was left until last. However, even after working on this issue for two days, no acceptable solution was developed that would meet the needs of the employees in both the Toronto and the Ottawa locations. A description of the problem is as follows.

Employees at Networking Solutions of Toronto had chosen not to have flex-time because many of these employees lived in the suburbs of Toronto. Living in the suburbs meant that they commuted to and from work on the GO trains, and/or used car pools. As there was often up to a 40-minute wait between trains, and/or they had to schedule their arrival and departure from work to fit with their car pool schedule, it meant that flex-time was not feasible. Therefore, instead of flex-time, the employees of Networking Solutions had negotiated two extra days per year that they could use for school, doctor appointments etc., without having to make up the time. Sure, flex-time works well in Ottawa, but we won't give in on this issue. The line was drawn in the sand. It is time to take a stand!

The president has decreed that there has to be one uniform policy for the new merged company. The transition team has 30 minutes to come up with options to solve this dilemma before presenting your solution to the new president and CEO of Networking Connections.

The Solution and Process

The first step is to write down the pros and cons of each option (flex-time versus two extra floating days off per year), see Figure 3-3. We then write

FIGURE 3-3

Options Pros and Cons Chart

First Policy Options: Flex-time	
Pros	**Cons**
• Consistency	• One party will feel disenfranchised
• Sets a precedent	• Unfair for some
• Unified solution	• Logistical problems
• Works well for some employees at Internet Connections	• Winners/losers

Second Policy Options: Floating Days Off	
Pros	**Cons**
• Consistency	• One party will feel disenfranchised
• Flexibility	• Harder to manage
• Sets a precedent	• Unfair for some
• Unified solution	• Us/them—lack of unity
• Works well for employees at Networking Solutions	• Winners/losers

down the pros of each option, in this case the pros of option one and the pros of option two together in one place, see Figure 3-4. At this point, options are generated that will maximize the list of combined pros.

FIGURE 3-4

Maximize the Pros—Pros from First and Second Options

- Consistency

- Sets a precedent

- Unified solution

- Flexibility

- Works well for employees at both Internet Connections and
  Networking Solutions

In this particular case, an option existed that would meet all of the pros in Figure 3-4. That option was to give all employees 15 hours of flex-time each year that they could use for doctor's appointments, etc., that they did not need to make up (consistency). The employees were also entitled to 37.5 hours of flex-time that had to be made up (flexibility/unified solution). The employees of both companies felt exceptionally fairly treated (win/win), and also felt that their previous organizations' cultures were honoured and validated, and the new company was beginning with a culture of creative solutions, honour and respect (precedent). Given how many mergers end up with terribly bad feelings on one or both sides and that the expected synergies from the mergers can fail to materialize, or take an inordinate amount of time to materialize, the decision made in this case was a very wise one and set a precedent of generating creative solutions for any type of difficult situation that may arise in the future. Exercise 3-2 provides an opportunity to practise pros and cons analysis on an issue with which you are currently faced.

EXERCISE 3-2

Pros and Cons Analysis

1. In the first two charts provided below, do a pros and cons analysis on a current problem that you are having.

First Policy Option	
Pros	**Cons**

Second Policy Option	
Pros	**Cons**

From *The Seven Strategies of Master Negotiators* by Brad McRae © 2002, McGraw-Hill Ryerson.

2. In the third policy option below, consolidate all of the pros from the various options completed in 1.

Third Policy Option

3. Finally, have a brainstorming session with several friends and/or colleagues and then develop a robust solution to satisfy as many of the pros as possible.

Step 7: Develop a Culture that Recognizes and Rewards Innovation

Up to this point, we have emphasized individuals who have developed creative and innovative solutions, which have enabled them to more effectively create value and to more effectively claim value. We should not lose sight of the fact that effective teams, departments and indeed, organizations as a whole, have learned to more effectively create and claim value. Examples of such innovative companies are: Maritime Life Assurance, Canadian National Railroad, Home Depot Canada and VanCity, among others.

Further examples of companies and organizations that do an excellent job of creating and claiming value can be found in some of the citations of the Resources of the Masters: An Annotated Bibliography.

The following excerpts from my interview with **Annette Verschuren**, president of Home Depot Canada, demonstrate the importance that her company places on developing a culture that recognizes and rewards innovative and creative solutions.

> *Recognition is one of the most important things that we can do*
>
> **Annette Verschuren**

B.M. *How have you developed a culture that recognizes and rewards innovative and creative solutions at Home Depot?*

A.V. We have created a culture at Home Depot that is very competitive. We have given a lot of autonomy to our store managers. We encourage innovation and we recognize people by promoting them. The cream does rise to the top, and the people who rise to the top are the best performers and the best performers are those who develop and encourage others. We put as much emphasis on the development of people as we do on return on investment.

Recognition is one of the most important things that we can do. I'm constantly making sure that if an associate finds a better way of doing something, we recognize them with customer service badges.

When an associate collects enough customer service badges, we send notes of encouragement, and after five customer service badges, they collect $100.

The greatest form of recognition is involvement in the growth of an organization. In the same way that our customers can say, "I laid this ceramic floor," there is a pride in doing good work at Home Depot. The other thing we really encourage is buying into the company through our stock option program. Thirty percent of our employees are shareholders, and they get a 15 percent discount when they purchase our company's stock. This is true for anyone who works for the company from day one. For example, I have an employee named Bill Bird. He started with Home Depot in the tool rental area. Through stock options, he has gained enough equity through this stock ownership program to purchase his retirement home. We have an option to help our people to dream and to dream big. The whole thing is based on merit. The harder they work, and the better the customer service, the more their stock, both literally and figuratively, will go up. Our culture is inherently merit based.

Lastly, that culture is talked about and encouraged. Those stories spread and people talk about those stories. And we need to encourage them, as leaders we have to get them to talk about them, to find them and to share them continually.

B.M. *You stated, "We put as much emphasis on the development of people as we do on return on investment," can you tell me about people development at Home Depot?*

A.V. There are two training programs, one at the store floor level and one at the managerial level. At the floor level, it's a 10-week process. Our responsibility is to transfer knowledge more than it is to sell products. We have a terrific facility and we make more of an investment in training than any other company, for example, there is cashier college, milling work college and flooring college 101, 102 and 103. A more specific example is our kitchen college, which is a very successful apprenticeship program in the design of and selling of kitchens. We also have an assistant manager and a manager development program. All of these programs are a very important part of our success—well-educated employees are worth a phenomenal amount.

We just keep raising the bar. Our objective to continually improve customer service levels and never let them diminish. The way to do that is to attract people, motivate people and invest in people.

At Home Depot Canada the building blocks of creating and claiming value can be seen on a daily basis. At the same time, it has created an organizational culture that is committed to recognizing that innovative solutions can be identified and put into action at all levels within an organization.

Creating and claiming value are two of the most essential strategies used by Master Negotiators. As most of us are inherently better at one of these skills than the other, it behoves us to do a careful analysis to determine on which strategy we most need to work. At the same time, we want to continue improving our more developed strategy. The tools set out in this Strategy and in the Master Negotiators' Preparation Form (Figure 2-1, in Strategy 2) are designed to do just that.

---

[1] *Harvard Business Review* (May-June 1997): 83-94.

[2] Maritime Medical Care and Blue Cross Atlantic merged to become Atlantic Blue Cross Care in 1998.

[3] This case study was developed by Brad McRae and Louise White of Maritime Life Assurance Co.

Strategy 4

Understand Negotiating Styles

I would say that my style leads to making long-term relationships work: where both parties feel that they got what they needed.

— *Isadore Sharp*

No matter how well-prepared you may be when entering negotiations, it can all fall apart if negotiating style—your own and your partner's—is not taken into account. This chapter covers seven factors that are central to understanding your own and your partner's negotiating style. These factors are:

1. identifying and understanding your negotiating style;
2. identifying and understanding your partner's negotiating style;
3. understanding the effectiveness of the various styles and combinations thereof;
4. identifying and controlling your shadow style;
5. identifying people who disguise their style;
6. using inclusiveness; and
7. using multiple skills simultaneously.

Your Negotiating Style

Your style and that of your partner's is critically important because it pervades every aspect of your negotiations. The best way to understand this is through the following analogy. We can think of a negotiation as a large ship on the ocean. The large ship would need a large rudder to properly steer it, and the ship would need a large set of hydraulic engines to move the rudder, and the large set of engines would take up valuable cargo space. I ask the participants in my courses how they would modify the large rudder so it would take smaller hydraulic engines to move it.

I always get some very innovative ideas like adding fins to the rudder, changing the rudder's shape, or making it more streamlined. The solution came from a brilliant German engineer named Antone Slettner who thought outside the box to add a small rudder, called a trim tab, to the larger rudder, see Figure 4-1. When the smaller rudder is turned, it builds up momentum, which makes it much easier to turn the larger rudder, hence smaller hydraulic engines are needed to turn the ship, which saves valuable cargo space.

The trim tab is analogous to our negotiating style, the larger rudder represents the negotiation, and the result or outcome of the negotiation is deter-

FIGURE 4-1

The Importance of Knowing Your Negotiating Style

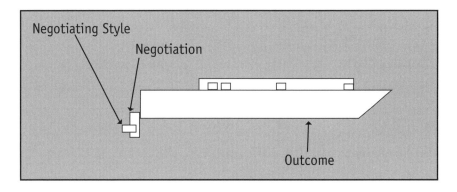

mined by the direction the ship is moving in. In other words, if we control our style, the trim tab, we have better control over the negotiation, the large rudder, and hence we have better control over the outcome of the negotiation. Therefore, it is imperative that we know what our negotiation style is and how to make it work for us rather than against us.

Your Partner's Negotiation Style

Please note that I used the word partner, not opponent or adversary. This is a vitally important distinction for three reasons. Firstly, if I view someone as an adversary or opponent, and if that person subsequently does something that is cooperative, I run the risk of not even seeing it and/or of discounting it because that behaviour does not fit with the way I have chosen to view the situation and/or the other party. In other words, I have to be vigilant both to create opportunities for cooperation and to clearly see and react positively to them when they are presented to me. The San Francisco rental car shuttle bus example cited in Strategy 1 is an excellent case in point.

The second reason why we need to pay close attention to the other party's negotiation style is richly illustrated by the following analogy. Assume that you are one of the world's best baseball players in terms of batting average. You can view the opposing pitcher as your adversary or you can view the opposing pitcher as your partner. If you view the opposing pitcher as your partner, you can then wait for your partner to pitch the perfect pitch so you can hit the perfect home run.

The application to negotiating is that if we view the other party as our partner, we can then look carefully as to how he or she uses language, metaphors and analogies to phrase his or her argument. We can also look for the underlying values that are important to the other party. By doing this, we can then make our points in their language, being mindful of their values. As a result, our partner is more readily able to hear what we have to say. This skill is a method of applying Stephen Covey's sage advice "Seek first to understand and then seek to be understood."[1]

The third reason is that there are times when we have to modify our preferred negotiation style to match the other party's style in order to get the other party to take us seriously. For example, if you are dealing with a hard bargainer, you may need to be phenomenally assertive in order for that person to treat you with any respect and credibility because that is the only style that that particular person understands. For example, although Major-General Lewis MacKenzie prefers to negotiate collaboratively, there were situations in Bosnia-Herzegovina where he had to initially use a great deal of power and force to get the warring factions to take him seriously, one instance being the beginning of the negotiations to reopen the Sarajevo airport. More will be said about the crucial importance of flexibility in the next section.

Effectiveness of Various Styles and Combinations

One of the very best sources of scientific information on negotiation style is the research on style and effectiveness by Gerald R. Williams[2] of the Faculty of Law at Brigham Young University. The main goal of this study was to identify the characteristics of highly effective negotiators. Using lawyers as his subjects, Williams found that there were three distinct primary negotiating styles or orientations: co-operative, competitive and no pattern.

The cooperative style is the quintessential win-win negotiator. The competitive negotiator is the quintessential win-as-much-as-you-can negotiator. The third pattern, no pattern, meant that there was no discernable pattern. Although many parties have somewhat mixed styles, it is important to look at the pure forms first, and to make the more subtle distinctions later.

It is also critically important to note that Williams not only identified the three primary styles, he also identified the fact that there were sub-categories in each category: effective, average and ineffective. Therefore, it is not enough to know what our style is; we also have to know how effectively we use our style. Knowing that you have a cooperative style is insufficient, for example, Williams has determined that 3 percent of the cooperatives were ineffective. They were gullible, naïve and frequently taken advantage of.

FIGURE 4-2

Percent of Attorneys in Each Category

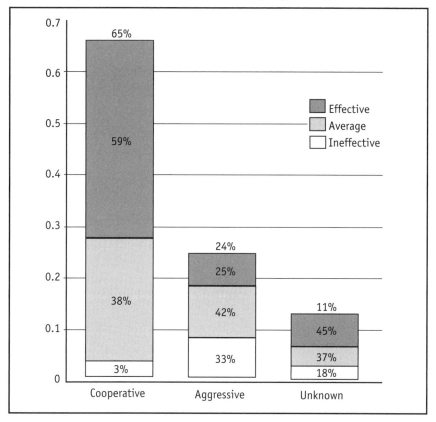

It should be noted that Williams replicated his study three times. The more times a study is replicated, the more confidence we can have in the results. Lastly, Williams postulates that the same findings apply to non-lawyers.[3] For a graphic representation of the percentage for effective, average and ineffective negotiators in each category, see Figure 4-2.

We need to learn the important distinctions between cooperative negotiators and competitive negotiators if we are to negotiate effectively with people who use these styles. The difference between these styles and the characteristics shared by both types of effective negotiators are summarized in Figure 4-3.

FIGURE 4-3

Styles of Effective Cooperative and Competitive Negotiators

Cooperative Objectives:	Competitive Objectives:
1. Conduct self ethically	1. Maximize settlement for client
2. Maximize settlement	2. Obtain profitable fee for self
3. Get a fair settlement	3. Outdo or outmanoeuvre opponent
Cooperative Traits:	**Competitive Traits:**
1. Trustworthy, ethical, fair	1. Dominating, forceful, attacking
2. Courteous, personable, tactful, sincere	2. Plans timing and sequence of actions (strategy), rigid, uncooperative
3. Fair minded	3. Carefully observes opponent
4. Realistic opening position	4. Unrealistic opening position
5. Accurately evaluates case	5. Clever
6. Does not use threats	6. Uses threats
7. Willing to share information	7. Reveals information gradually
8. Skillfully probes [partner's interests]	

Traits Shared by Both Types of Effective Negotiators:

1. Prepared
2. Honest, ethical
3. Perceptive/skillful in reading cues
4. Takes satisfaction in using their negotiating skills
5. Realistic, reasonable, rational, analytical
6. Creative
7. Flexible/adaptable/versatile
8. Convincing
9. Self-controlled

Materials for Master Class on Mediation and Negotiation, June 1995, Gerald R. Williams, p. 35.

EFFECTIVE COOPERATIVES

Effective cooperatives are quintessential "win-win" negotiators who focus on mutual gains. They are creative problem solvers and want a good outcome where all of the parties can consider that they were treated fairly. They would like all sides to feel good about the outcome, the relationships between the parties and the process used to arrive at that outcome. Effective cooperatives are able to both create and claim value and are flexible. In addition, they are able to use power effectively if necessary. In sum, they are strategically cooperative.

INEFFECTIVE COOPERATIVES

If effective cooperatives are strategically cooperative, ineffective cooperatives are unconditionally cooperative. In other words, they are cooperative both when it makes sense to be so, but also when it does not. They are consistently too trustful. Synonyms for too trustful include terms like gullible, naïve and easily exploited. The second major factor that differentiated effective cooperatives from their ineffective counterparts was that the ineffective cooperatives were too "gentle, obliging, patient, and forgiving . . . no matter what happens, they are going to be polite and courteous, and [forgiving] and try to get along with you."[4]

In sum, ineffective cooperatives are not good at claiming value for themselves and, because they are so trusting and so forgiving, they encourage others to claim value against them. Ineffective cooperatives therefore are frequently taken advantage of.

EFFECTIVE COMPETITIVES

Effective competitive negotiators are the quintessential "win as much as you can" negotiators. They want to be the winner and claim most, if not all, of the value.

Effective competitives come to the table incredibly well-prepared and are flexible. This means that although they try to win the negotiation by being aggressive and well-prepared, if that strategy turns out not to work because they are dealing with another effective negotiator, no matter what the style of that other negotiator—that is, competitive, cooperative or no pattern—they have the flexibility and ability to collaborate and/or compromise, because getting a deal is better than not getting a deal. In other words, although effective competitives place more emphasis on claiming value, they are flexible enough to create value if the situation warrants it.

INEFFECTIVE COMPETITIVES

Ineffective competitives use their style solely to intimidate and bluff their way through the negotiation because they are, in fact, ill-prepared. The ineffective competitives have very little flexibility and when faced with a strategy that is not working, maintain or increase the level of aggression. The common result is that the negotiation breaks off, the deal remains unmade, and the relationship between the parties is damaged. Because of their inflexibility, they see the world only in terms of opponents. They only know how to claim value and they tend to be poor at seeing the larger picture or seeing outside-the-box solutions; hence they are very poor at creating value. In fact, Williams found that ineffective competitives were so demanding that others typically found them to be obnoxious, and hence would prefer to avoid them altogether rather than negotiate with them if they could possibly help it. Ineffective competitives usually employ a take-it-or-leave-it strategy.

Williams rightly recommends that we consciously "learn to recognize these patterns, to understand how they operate, to know when they are likely to be productive and when they are counterproductive, and most important, perhaps, how to deal with [negotiators who use] each of the patterns."[5] The reason we have to do this consciously is to correct for our natural tendency to assume that all negotiators work from the same set of assumptions that we do. Williams' research is summarized in Figure 4-4.

NEGOTIATING COMBINATIONS

One way to further examine these patterns is to look at what happens when the various types of negotiators negotiate in pairs. Consider the following combinations:

FIGURE 4-4

Characteristics of Effective and Ineffective Negotiators by Style

Cooperative Style Effective	Competitive Style Effective
Healers/Transformers/ Creative Problem Solvers	Warrior

Cooperative Style Ineffective	Competitive Style Ineffective
Naïve/ Gullible/Too idealistic/ Unsure of self/Lacking in confidence/Obliging/Patsy/Mark/ Frequently taken advantage of/ Easy target/Soft touch/Easy prey/Sucker/Push over	Headstrong/Intolerant/Impatient/ Rigid/Demanding/Unreasonable/ Uncooperative/Arrogant/Tactless/ Devious/Conniving/Unskilled in reading cues/Bluffer/Unwilling to share information/Quarrelsome/ Rude/Hostile/Obstructive/ Unrealistic/Positional/Uses a narrow range of strategies

1. Cooperative negotiator versus cooperative negotiator.
2. Competitive negotiator versus competitive negotiator.
3. Cooperative negotiator versus competitive negotiator.

It is possible to predict some general tendencies from each of these combinations.

Effective Cooperative Negotiating with Same

Effective cooperative and effective cooperative is a match made in heaven. If the problem has a creative, mutual gain solution, they will find it.

Effective Competitive Negotiating with Same

In a way, you might expect a brawl. But this often is not the case; although there is a higher risk of breakdown and the negotiation will take longer and consume more resources, the negotiators do speak the same language and do understand one another. "[And because they can be flexible, they are] . . . perfectly capable of cooperating with one another if they are convinced that is the better way to proceed."[6]

Effective Cooperative and Effective Competitive

[This] combination is at the root of the majority of problems in negotiation, because these two negotiators do not speak the same language; they do not understand one another. They are operating on contrary assumptions.

[Cooperative] negotiators are trustworthy, ethical, and fair; they want a fair outcome; they adopt realistic positions; they avoid the use of threats; they disclose the facts early; and they value the prospect of agreement. In other words, cooperatives are problem solvers. How do they solve problems? On the merits; their instinct is to lay the facts out on the table. If I am a cooperative negotiator and I lay out my facts, and if you are cooperative, and you lay out your facts, then the two of us, as objective, fair-minded adults, can solve any problem. This is how cooperatives see their task. Against other cooperatives, this works very well. And since 65% of the negotiators in our study are basically cooperative, a cooperative will face another cooperative about 66% of the time.

But competitive negotiators do not see themselves primarily as problem solvers, at least not in the same sense as cooperatives. They are warriors. Their strategy assumes the other side is an enemy to be attacked and defeated and their strategy is well adapted to that end. They are dominating, forceful, and attacking; they adopt more extreme positions; they use threats; they are reluctant to reveal information; and they seek a victory over the other side.

Which is the better strategy? Of course, we all prefer our own. Cooperatives feel their way is better; competitives have no doubt it is their own. In my opinion they are both wrong, because when you need a problem solver or a healer nothing else will quite do, and when you really need a warrior, it is also true that nothing else will do. We cannot escape the reality that they are both legitimate and, in their time, indispensable. The question is not, Which strategy should I invariably use? but rather: How can I develop sufficiently as a negotiator that I can appropriately invoke one or the other, depending on the requirements of the situation? I have come to believe that a fully developed negotiator should be capable of appropriately adopting either one in the proper circumstances.[7]

What does all of this research tell us about negotiating? Firstly, we need to know our own primary style, cooperative or competitive. Secondly, we need to examine how our style works with people who use a similar style. For example, if we are a cooperative negotiating with another cooperative, where does our style work for us, and where does it work against us? Or if we are a competitive negotiating with another competitive, where does our style work for us and where does it work against us?

Perhaps the most interesting aspect of researching our own negotiating style's effectiveness will be our comparisons when we negotiate with someone who uses a style different from our preferred style. For example, if we are a competitive negotiator paired with a cooperative or a cooperative negotiator paired with a competitive, we need to know where our style works and where we need to make changes in the way we negotiate. By accurately identifying our own style of negotiating as well as identifying the style of the person with whom we are negotiating, we are much more likely to negotiate effectively. We are also much more likely to make informed choices during the negotiation process and, therefore, much more likely to negotiate outcomes that are favourable.

Identifying and Controlling Your Shadow Style

The term "shadow style" refers to a more primitive negotiation style that comes into play when we get emotionally hooked. When we get emotionally hooked, we allow strong emotions to cloud our preferred style, and we negotiate less well than we could or should. The following is an excellent example of how we get emotionally hooked. Jack is the father of two great kids. When Jack was growing up, he found a few things that his parents said really annoyed him. Jack swore that he would never behave in a similar manner with his own children. For example, Jack decided that he would never use guilt to get his children to eat everything on their plates. Then one day, when everything that could have gone wrong at work went wrong and Jack's self-esteem and frustration tolerance level were at an all-time low, he came home from work and the children were at him from the moment he opened the door. He sat down at the dinner table vowing to have a relaxing meal with his spouse and offspring. The children complained about the perfectly good food on their plates, picking at this and trying to hide that, moving more food than they were eating, and then all of a sudden, those very words that Jack swore would never be spoken in his household—about the starving children in less fortunate parts of the world—passed his lips. This scenario graphically illustrates the process of becoming emotionally hooked with our shadow style coming to the forefront.

Our shadow negotiating style can rear its head just as easily at work as at home. For example, John's preferred style is to be warm, open and congenial, however, when he is overly tired or has very strong feelings about an issue, his shadow style is to be overly aggressive; he becomes Attila the Hun. Our shadow style can be responsible for breaking off, giving in or escalating a conflict. It is important not only to improve our primary style, but also to better control our shadow style.

In summary, our shadow style comes into play when we become emotionally hooked. When uncontrolled emotions become involved, we can lose self-control and negotiate in a manner that is detrimental to the substantive outcome we wish to establish, to the relationships with the other party, or both.

In general, when we become emotionally hooked, our shadow style is to become too aggressive, too passive, or too passive-aggressive.

ISADORE SHARP, EFFECTIVE COOPERATIVE NEGOTIATOR

Effective cooperative negotiators achieve an ideal balance in terms of the substantive outcome, the relationship(s) and the process by which the negotiation takes place. The following interview with Master Negotiator **Isadore Sharp** demonstrates this balance. Isadore is the founder, president and CEO of one of the world's most admired luxury hotels, the Four Seasons.

B.M. *Please describe your negotiating style.*

I.S. I would say that my style leads to making long-term relationships work; where both parties feel that they got what they needed. I try to understand what the other party needs and to keep in mind what we need. I learned that you cannot be intransigent, you have to be open. I try to be sensitive to other party's needs by not putting forth a position that leads to an arrogance of knowing it all.

B.M. *How did you develop your style?*

I.S. Over time, I learned the skills in dealing with people in a manner that enabled us to continue the discussion.

> *I try to be sensitive to other party's needs by not putting forth a position that leads to an arrogance of knowing it all.*
>
> **Isadore Sharp**

B.M. *Can you give me an example?*

I.S. When I opened my first hotel on Jarvis St. in downtown Toronto, I had an idea that I wanted to try out. That idea was to combine what was best in a motel with a hotel that was literally downtown. It took me five years of knocking on doors to get someone to look at it, and that was my start in the hotel business.

B.M. *How did you learn to use your style effectively?*

I.S. A lot of it had to do with how much belief you have in what you are doing. It is subliminal, something that you truly believe is the right thing, and then get others to believe in your belief.

B.M. *Can you give me an example?*

I.S. The example I am thinking of . . . is on the concept for the Inn on the Park in London [England], which is now The Four Seasons - London. It was most important and held significant impact because of the historical background it had on the development of the Four Seasons Hotels. It set the direction for the company. It also gave me an understanding of how important trust and respect is in sustaining long-term relationships.

It was my third hotel, so I didn't have much of a background in the industry. A representative of the McAlpine family was interested in building a mid-range hotel of 350 rooms in London, and the hotel was in the planning stages at the time I made an offer. The problem was that I wasn't interested in the type of hotel that they wanted to build. So I offered them a deal. I would be responsible for the business operation. It would take up the same space but would have significantly fewer rooms. At the time, all of the consultants said I couldn't do that because London already had a lot of luxury hotels. They called me the crazy Canadian. I explained that the hotel that I wanted to build would cost less to build.

That negotiation took five years. We started in 1964 and the hotel opened in 1970. Years later I asked the gentleman, who was now a Lord, how he had the courage to make this business deal when he knew that I was so new to the business. He said, "My dear boy, over time in dealing with people, you develop a belief and a trust and that becomes your best guide."

B.M. *So, the Four Seasons London was a touchstone.*

I.S. Yes. We created a small boutique hotel. At the same time, we built a 1,600 room convention hotel in Toronto with ITT Sheraton. It was the contrast of the small boutique hotel with the 1,600 room convention hotel that was the beginning of the Four Seasons' culture.

B.M. *Can you tell me more about the Four Seasons' culture?*

I.S. If I could reconstruct the history of the culture over the last 40 years, there were several milestones. The first was to operate only medium sized luxury hotels. The other decisions and culture evolved out of that. Secondly, we would differentiate ourselves by the service. The third decision also dealt with the culture. If we were interested in making service our competitive advantage, our corporate mission statement, our goals, our beliefs and our vision must reflect service. The one line that meant the most was that we should "treat people by the golden rule," and it has been stringently observed. One of the most painful things I had to do was to terminate several of our most senior people because they couldn't "walk the talk." That culture has to permeate throughout the organization, from the top to the base of the triangle.

> *I can only sell what I truly believe in, and therefore in negotiation you have to be able to think on your feet and that is only possible if you know what you truly believe in.*
>
> **Isadore Sharp**

Isadore Sharp ended the interview by saying: "I can only sell what I truly believe in, and therefore in negotiation you have to be able to think on your feet and that is only possible if you know what you truly believe in."

BUZZ HARGROVE, EFFECTIVE COMPETITIVE NEGOTIATOR

Most people know from the media that the president of the Canadian Auto Workers, **Buzz Hargrove**, is a tough negotiator. In 1996, Canadian Airlines International was in considerable financial difficulty. Buzz and the CAW were under incredible pressure to make additional wage concessions to "keep the company flying." Five other unions had already made concessions, Buzz held firm, which forced the provincial and federal governments to make concessions. It was a pure case of who would blink first and it wasn't going to be Buzz Hargrove and the CAW. Using Gerald Williams' research on the styles and characteristics of effective negotiators, Buzz would be classified as an excellent example of a very effective, strategic competitive negotiator.

I had the pleasure of interviewing Buzz Hargrove in May, 2001. He spoke incredibly quickly, with great enthusiasm and had a wealth of data and anecdotes at his disposal.

B.M. *Describe your style as a negotiator.*

B.H. My style is to be tough, but also to be pragmatic enough to know if an agreement is there, we will get it. I was first elected as president of the union in 1992, and that was the first time that we had agreements with all of the big three automobile manufacturers without a strike. We did the same thing in 1999.

> *I prefer to come to the table incredibly well-prepared, build the expectations high, and roll back if necessary.*
>
> **Buzz Hargrove**

I am tough on issues that are important to us. If there is a perception of weakness we will lose every time. Therefore, I prefer to come to the table incredibly well-prepared, build the expectations high, and roll back if necessary.

In terms of bargaining, I view the world as long-term—and that is true wherever I negotiate—the automobile industry, government or aerospace. I see no advantage to seeing any party take advantage over a short-run situation, because it comes back to haunt you in the long run. Therefore, I take a long-term view with relationships and that is part of my success.

I learned this from watching others, that is, watching at how collective bargaining works on both sides of the table. If one party has a temporary advantage over the other and takes advantage of that party, it is like building a time bomb for the future, for example, when Chrysler forced an unnecessary cutback of $1.15 an hour on us in 1980. In 1982 we had a five-week strike to get the $1.15 back. My style is one of looking long-term.

Equally important to Buzz is the need to balance toughness with being pragmatic as the following except from his book *Labour of Love* points out.

Some of my critics like to call me "the labour boss who rattles the boardrooms"—as if my only intention is to be stubborn and force a strike on management. That's absurd. I'm better known in labour-management circles as a person who knows how to reach a settlement by reading the situation and moving demands around on the table until the deal begins to look too sweet for the employers to pass up. Our goal is always to get a deal our members can be happy with. I learned that from people like Ken Gerard, Dennis McDermott, and [Bob] White.[8]

B.M. *How important is flexibility in the negotiating process?*

B.H. Flexibility is a misused word. My personal style is that you have to go in tough, and management has to be convinced that [they have to be part of finding] a solution to the problem that was raised. I like to go out on a limb and bring the management person with me, but I have the saw and they have to work with me. In most cases management has 90 percent of the power—so we have to be prepared to take risks. So far, no management has ever come to the table and said we are making a lot of money and we would like to talk to you about how to share it.

I argue as much with our own team as I do with the company. We have to get our committee on side with the issues. We also have to be pragmatic and this means that some of our aspiration may not be achievable.

Another of my overriding principles is to communicate, communicate and communicate some more. In negotiation, sometimes people get positional on who has to call whom first. This is a colossal waste of time. I just pick up the phone and say, "Let's talk."

What most people haven't seen and don't know about, is Buzz Hargrove's equally tough and successful negotiating within the union, particularly on the issue of inclusiveness—that the union should include, represent and respect all of its members including visible minorities, women, the physically challenged, and gays and lesbians.

B.M. *How did you come to develop your strong views on inclusiveness?*

B.H. A lot of it had to do with growing up with my sister Mildred who had polio and watching how cruelly treated she was as a child. I also saw how she developed herself to her fullest potential in spite of the limitations that others tried to place on her because she was different. Where we grew up in rural New Brunswick, kids that were different have a very hard go at it. We lived in a pretty macho part of the world. . . . [t]he only people who were different were people who looked different or had a disability. People were cruel to my sister. I watched her bounce back in spite of this. She was an excellent swimmer and that worked well in spite of having only one arm and one leg that worked. She showed what she could do in spite of what others thought. That is a lesson that has always stuck with me.

Today we have done an enormous amount of work in this area, for example we have to write about gay and lesbian issues, we have same-sex spousal benefits, and we have a gay and lesbian conference once a year. For example, there are few people who are more macho than miners are, and yet we negotiated same-sex spousal benefits. This is an issue we have taken on in the union. It is one of those things we have to fight every day. People not only have to say that our union includes women, people of colour, and gays at all levels within the union—our action must support our words.

At times when CEOs are being paid more and more, regardless of how well their company or organization is doing, all Canadians deserve to prosper, to have decent pensions, daycare facilities and medical coverage.

B.M. *What is the importance of being a life-long learner?*

B.H. Every day is a learning experience, and every set of negotiations is different. It is also important to note that the individuals at the table play such an incredibly important role. There have been more strikes over personalities than issues at the table. Negotiators have to learn to become experts at human relations, experts at coming up with options and experts at knowing when and when not to negotiate. For example, the chief negotiator at General Motors would never agree to same-sex spousal benefits—even if it meant a prolonged strike. GM had to fire him so we could get an agreement. Knowing the psychology of the parties with whom you will negotiate and knowing clearly when not to negotiate are incredibly important. That's why we must be life-long learners. You also have to enjoy what you do. Some people find it stressful; I thrive on it.

Perhaps Ontario Labour Minister Chris Stockwell summed up the value that Buzz Hargrove brings to the table best when he said, "I look at a guy like Buzz Hargrove and the work he does. At $139,000 a year, I think Buzz is worth every nickel of that $139,000, every last nickel."

We could see from Gerald Williams's research that only one out of four people can use the effective competitive style of negotiation effectively. Buzz Hargrove can, because like all effective competitive negotiators, he comes to the table incredibly well-prepared, he can be flexible when the situation warrants it, he keeps his eye on the prize, and he negotiates just as strongly inside the union as out. There is one aspect of negotiation style that we have not covered yet, and that is what happens when your negotiation counterpart tries to lull you into complacency by disguising his or her style.

Identifying People who Disguise their Style

Being an expert witness is one of the most daunting tasks anyone can face. Often the process is extremely adversarial. When it is time to be cross-examined, the opposing lawyer will often try to discredit the witness personally, in addition to their testimony. Nowhere is it more important to be well-prepared, to practise self-control and to identify as thoroughly and as early as possible the negotiation style of the person who will be cross-examining you. The following example illustrates the use of these three important skills in identifying the disguised negotiating style.

I am a registered psychologist and have a very small private practice. I met "William"[9] five years ago when he was referred to me during the break-up of his marriage due to irreconcilable differences. There were two young children involved and his ex-wife had custody with liberal visitation rights for William. Although it was a very difficult time for him, William worked hard and was very pro-active at maintaining an excellent relationship with his children. After a suitable period of time the counselling sessions came to an appropriate ending.

I was surprised when I received a telephone call from William three and a half years later. He had been off work for six months and was suffering from very ill health, allegedly from being exposed to toxic chemicals at work. William sought and received exceptional medical treatment from his primary physician and a number of specialists to whom he was referred. I saw him in my role as counsellor as he tried to deal with the psychological uncertainty in trying to deal with his medical problems. William was eventually terminated from work and his case was scheduled to go to arbitration. I was asked to testify as an expert witness.

William had excellent legal representation. His lawyers, hired by the union, were articulate, well informed and very well-prepared. The union's lead lawyer thought I would be on the stand for two hours defending my psychological report. He also cross-examined me in a simulation where he played the role of the other side's lawyer to help prepare me for what often turns out to be quite an ordeal.

As it turned out, I was not on the stand for two hours, I was on the stand for eight. My original assessment of the situation was that the tribunal was there to look at the most accurate information possible to arrive at the closest approximation of the truth, and that all parties should and would endeavour to use the most constructive and collaborative manner possible.

The opposing lawyer, we will call her Martha, represented the organization that had terminated William. She appeared to be very congenial and cooperative. She was polite, courteous, soft-spoken and well mannered. My first supposition was that she was a cooperative negotiator.

I then noticed that she started all of her questions with the phrase, "I'm sure you would agree that ... ." I soon realized that if she used this phrase for all of her questions, and if I did disagree, it would not be too long before I started to sound and look disagreeable.

I then asked the chief arbitrator if I could have the question framed in a more neutral way so I would be able to freely agree or disagree after I heard the question. The chief arbitrator said that opposing counsel was entitled to phrase her questions any way she wished and that my point had been noted.

Martha then got to work in earnest. She asked if I would not agree that divorce, especially divorce where children were involved, was stressful. I knew from the question that she was trying to blame my client's condition on the stress of going through a separation and divorce and not on the alleged environmental poisoning. I replied that although this was true in most cases, I have known of some clients who were ecstatic at the prospect of being divorced.

As stated earlier in this book, the Master Negotiator's secret formula is to always expect the unexpected. I had known that one psychiatrist had assessed my client, but I did not know that a second psychiatrist had assessed him. Both reports stated that my client was suffering from an acute stress disorder. The organization's lawyer introduced the psychiatric reports by stating that both psychiatrists had exemplary reputations in their field, which they did. She then stated that she was sure that I would disagree with their diagnosis. I knew that once again I was being set up.

I then stated that, on the contrary, I would agree with my colleagues' diagnosis with one exception. With that I started to reach for my copy of the *Diagnostic and Statistical Manual of Mental Disorders—Fourth Edition* (DSM-IV),[10] which is the standard assessment guide in the field of mental health, published by the American Psychiatric Association. The opposing lawyer said that my opinion would suffice and I did not need the DSM-IV. Martha telling me I didn't need to refer to the DSM-IV, strongly reinforced my supposition that I should use it. Since she herself had referred to the diagnostic manual, and since I was testifying as an expert witness, the chief arbitrator affirmed my right to quote from the DSM-IV.

What Martha did not predict was that I had done my homework. I was able to point out that although the psychiatrists said my client's diagnosis was "acute," that is a disorder lasting less than six months, I, on the other hand, stated that his condition was "chronic," that is the disturbance lasted for six months or longer, so that therefore, the true cause of my client's distress was the uncertainty he was suffering due to the alleged environmental toxicity. I further added, that if the two well respected psychiatrists had had the luxury of seeing my client for more than one visit, I was sure that their diagnosis would agree with mine.

The opposing lawyer was flummoxed and had difficulty formulating subsequent questions and locating some of her material, all of which did not happen when she heard answers she was prepared to hear. In other words, she helped make my client's case.

On the surface she appeared to be a very cordial cooperative negotiator. Underneath, she was a competitive negotiator, and a somewhat ineffective one at that, because she came to the hearing inadequately prepared. The lesson learned and reinforced is that Master Negotiators come to the table incredibly well-prepared, not only on content, but also in their ability to diagnose their counterpart's style and have the ability to act and react accordingly.

Inclusiveness

An important element of style that is almost always overlooked in articles, books and seminars on negotiation is inclusiveness. Inclusiveness has to do with the issue of who should be at the negotiating table and/or the failure to build the necessary strategic alliances that are necessary to bring a particular agreement to fruition. As mentioned earlier, Buzz Hargrove, president of the CAW, has used the principle of inclusiveness extremely effectively when negotiating within the union with respect to membership issues.

Overlooking inclusiveness is one of the most common mistakes that amateur negotiators make, and it can be a costly one. Most Canadians remember the failure of the Meech Lake Accord to amend the Canadian Constitution; the First Nations felt excluded from the process. The cost of this failure was seeing Elijah Harper vote no in the Manitoba Legislature. A second example is the Canadian government's hepatitis C compensation plan. The plan was to compensate some of the people who had contracted hepatitis C through blood products and transfusions. However, it did not include all who had contracted hepatitis C and left out those infected with HIV. Janet Conners fought long and hard to have people who were tragically infected with HIV through tainted blood transfusions fairly compensated (see Strategy 6 for Janet Conners' story). In both of these cases, those who were excluded prevailed in the court of public opinion and the government looked bad.

An excellent example of the consequences of exclusion is the conflict between the Cree of Northern Quebec and Hydro-Québec and the government of Quebec over the Great Whale hydroelectric project in northern Quebec, also known as James Bay II.

Hydro-Québec and the Province of Quebec vs. the Cree

On Earth Day in April 1990, a group of Cree, one of the two indigenous people of the James Bay peninsula of northern Quebec, paddled down the Hudson River in a native vessel called an Odeyak. They had portaged the craft across the winter snows of northern Quebec to Montreal. For six weeks they paddled, until they reached New York City. That trip plus follow-up public relations efforts over the next several months garnered support from more than 100 organizations including the Sierra Club, Greenpeace, and the National Audubon Society. (Susskind and Field, p. 160).

Thus began the battle surrounding James Bay II between the Cree and Hydro-Québec and the province of Quebec. Hydro-Québec had built a mega hydro-electric complex in northern Quebec on the James Bay River in the 1970s. The project would generate millions of dollars in the sale of electricity to the power hungry New England States. A second phase, known as James Bay II or the Great Whale Project, was planned.

However, based on their experience with James Bay I, the Cree were very concerned about environmental problems such as mercury poisoning, health problems such as increased obesity and heart disease, and social problems such as alcohol and spousal abuse, unemployment and high suicide rates all of which had resulted from the first James Bay project. The Cree were alarmed that these problems would become even more widespread if James Bay II were to be developed.

The Cree started a very successful public relations campaign that effectively stopped James Bay II. A canoe journey to New York City brought the Cree's concerns to the attention of major American environmental groups, the media, and state and federal governments. The full extent of the Cree's public relations campaign can be illustrated by the "Ban the Dam Jam for James Bay" concert, held in 1991 in New York City. Lastly, the Cree also presented their case to the United Nations Commission on Human Rights and to the International Water Tribunal Foundation in Amsterdam and to the mayors of New York City, Burlington, Vermont and several other municipalities.

To make matters worse, Hydro-Québec and the province of Quebec refused to participate in a federal environmental review, which made them look arrogant and as if they were pushing their agenda without taking the concerns of the Cree and the environmentalists seriously. Chief of the First Nations Assembly, Ovid Mercredi, pointed out that the government of Quebec, which was championing the protection of French language and French culture, ended up denigrating the importance of the Cree language and the Cree culture. The irony of this situation was widely reported in the media.

The James Bay II project was put on hold indefinitely, and a 20-year, $5-billion contract between the New York Power Authority and Hydro-Québec was cancelled.

Susskind and Field concluded that the inflexibility of the Quebec government and of Hydro-Québec "encouraged the Cree to seek alliances in the United States and Europe." In time, Hydro-Québec found itself facing an international array of opponents ranging from the New York Power Authority to international tribunals (Susskind and Field, p. 177). This example is a strong illustration of how negotiating styles and the lack of inclusiveness can change the course and affect the outcome of a negotiation.

Mathew Coon Come and Ovid Mercredi knew the power of developing strategic alliances, and influencing and recruiting powerful outside voices to their cause. They also masterfully utilized the power of commitment, the power of public relations and the power of the media. For readers who would like a more in-depth understanding of this case, see Susskind and Field's classic book *Dealing with an Angry Public: The Mutual Gains Approach to Resolving Disputes.*

In summary, Master Negotiators always ask themselves, their constituents and their advisors whether there is anyone who is not included at the table, and who needs to be included to bring the negotiations and agreements to fruition. Master Negotiators also have the flexibility to include parties who become identified as integral to the negotiation, even after the negotiation process has begun. More will be said about the importance of building strategic alliances in Strategy 6.

Using Multiple Skills Simultaneously

One sign of a true Master Negotiator is the ability to use several skills and strategies simultaneously. An excellent example of a Master Negotiator who uses multiple skills simultaneously is **Paul Tellier**, president and CEO of the Canadian National Railroad.

Historically, the Canadian National Railroad (CN) and the Canadian Pacific Railroad (CP) were east coast to west coast railroads. All that changed dramatically with the advent of the North American Free Trade Agreement. CN bought the Illinois Central Railroad, which transformed CN from an east to west, to both an east-west and a north-south railroad. In fact, today more than 50 percent of CN's revenue is based on north-south as opposed to east-west traffic.

Capitalizing on growth opportunities and economies of scale, CN and Burlington Northern Santa Fe (BNSF) Railroads announced plans to merge, thereby becoming the largest railroad in North America. However, this merger would require regulatory approval in both Canada and the United States. Eventually, for regulatory and nationalist reasons, the merger plans fell through in July, 2000. Paul Tellier's reaction to the failed merger was, "Canadian National Railway Company's failed efforts to build the largest railway in North America were a disappointment but not a distraction."

B.M. *How did you react to the failed merger?*

P.T.   My colleagues, staff and even the board were expecting me to be
bitter, depressed or angry. My reaction was to turn the page and look
for other strategic options. The board couldn't believe I could
bounce back so soon. My experience in life is that when the going
is easy, many people are able to provide leadership. It's when the
going gets tough, this is where leadership is required. We have
22,000 employees; soon to be 24,000. I couldn't afford to say that
I wouldn't be in top form for a period of days or weeks.

It also helps to know that we have a fall back position or positions. When we were trying to orchestrate the merger with BNSF I
knew that the chances were 50/50. However, at the same time we
were trying to manage a combination of different possibilities,
including the possibility of sharing train track with CP in Western
Canada, and this was at the same time CP was fiercely opposed to
the merger. One of my cardinal rules is that we had to make sure
that we were making progress on all fronts. Therefore, when we made
the decision to abort [the] BNSF merger, we were able to proceed, in
a week or 10 days with the joint initiative with CP. The joint initiative with CP will result in bottom-line growth of about $30 million
per year. These savings will accrue because both railroads will share
track in western Canada. When the announcement of our joint initiative with CP was made, the market gave us a lot of credit for
reacting very quickly.

There is no doubt that Paul Tellier is one of Canada's Master Negotiators. The
above example vividly illustrates how a Master Negotiator uses multiple skills
simultaneously, in this case, the skills of preparation, flexibility, self-control
and building strategic alliances.

For the reader who is interested in leadership, vision, and the negotiating, influencing, and flexibility necessary to consistently bring about positive results, keep an eye on Paul Tellier. In the meantime, I highly recommend Exercise 4-1 to help you identify other Master Negotiators who use multiple skills simultaneously.

Marshall McLuhan said that the "medium is the message." In a very real sense, in a negotiation the style is the message. In Strategy 4 we covered the critical importance of knowing your own negotiating style and steps you can take to improve it. We also examined the importance of knowing the other party's style, and the value of flexibility, self-control, inclusiveness and the ability to use multiple skills simultaneously to make sure you use your style as effectively as possible. In Strategy 5, we will turn our attention to effectively managing the negotiation process.

---

[1] Stephen R. Covey. *The 7 Habits of Highly Effective People: Powerful Lessons in Personal Change.* New York: Simon & Schuster, 1989.

[2] "Styles and effectiveness in negotiation." In *Negotiation: Strategies for Mutual Gain.* Lavinia Hall, (ed.). Newbury Park, California: Sage Publications, pp. 151-174.

[3] I do not have any empirical evidence concerning these matters among non-lawyer populations, but my personal experience is that all people, from home-makers to real estate salespersons to MBA students find that the results speak to them at least as powerfully as they do to lawyers and law students. In fact, I have been teaching the same course on negotiation at the BYU Business School as I do at the law school, and they seem to fit perfectly. Personal correspondence from Professor Williams, June, 2001.

[4] Williams, *supra*, note 2, at p. 162.

[5] Ibid., at p. 161.

[6] Ibid., at p. 164.

[7] Ibid., at pp. 164-65.

[8] Buzz Hargrove with Wayne Skeene. *Labour of Love—The Fight to Create a More Humane Canada.* Toronto: MacFarlane Walter & Ross, 1988, at p. 71.

[9] Client's name changed.

[10] American Psychiatric Assn. Washington, D.C.: American Psychiatric Assn., 1994. This was replaced in 2000 by DSM-IV-TR.

EXERCISE 4-1

Multiple Skills

Write the names of three people that you know or know of who demonstrate the use of the multiple skills such as leadership, visioning, effective
communication skills, effective negotiating and influencing skills and/or
the use of flexibility.

1. _____

   _____

2. _____

   _____

3. _____

   _____

What are some of the lessons that you learned or can learn by carefully
observing how the above three people bring about positive results?

_____

_____

_____

_____

_____

_____

_____

_____

From *The Seven Strategies of Master Negotiators* by Brad McRae © 2002, McGraw-Hill Ryerson.

STRATEGY 5

Manage the Negotiation Process

Rather than worry too much about outcomes, it is better to focus our attention on the process. After all, once you have your outcome, it is too late to do anything about it. So I recommend becoming an expert not on outcomes, but rather on the process by which they are arrived at.

Gerald Williams[1]

We can think of negotiation as analogous to a three-legged stool. One leg of the stool represents the substantive outcome, the second leg of the stool represents the people and the type of relationship they will have, and the third leg of the stool represents the process which the parties will use to reach an agreement (see Figure 5-1). If any of the legs does not measure up, the stool becomes unstable and potentially useless. It is up to the negotiator to ensure that the processes are monitored and kept moving towards optimal performance.

Managing the negotiation process means exploring the critical importance of:

1. paying close attention to the substantive outcome, the relationship outcome and the negotiation process;
2. choice points; and
3. the diagnostic, formula and details stages of the negotiating process

Strategy 5 will also detail 12 strategies and techniques that Master Negotiators use to keep the process focused and moving forward.

FIGURE 5-1

Negotiations in Terms of Substance, Relationship and Process

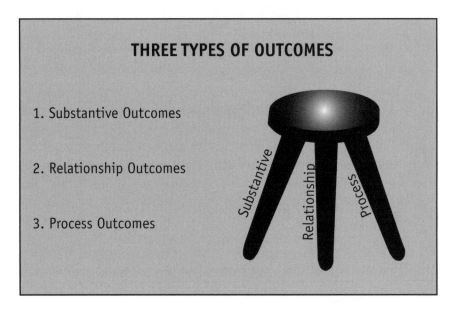

Three Types of Outcomes

Less experienced negotiators will focus entirely on the substantive outcome. If the process is terrible or the relationships get damaged, so be it. That is, until there is another negotiation, and that negotiation becomes more difficult due to the previous interaction.

More experienced negotiators focus on both the substantive outcome and on the people and their relationships. These negotiators want a good substantive outcome and a good relationship outcome.

Master Negotiators focus on all three elements, that is, the substantive outcome, the people and the type of relationships they will have, and on choosing the most effective negotiation process for each and every negotiation situation. Each of these three elements inherently affects the other as the following example illustrates.

My daughter attended a French immersion school in Halifax. This school provides an incredibly close community not only for the children, but also for the parents. However, like most school boards, the Halifax Regional School Board was facing a number of funding and debt-related issues. Some underutilized schools were going to close and every possible step was needed to save money.

During this time, a school board official decided that the Board could save money by taking one of the two Grade 6 teachers out of our school. The major problem that this caused was that the maximum legislated class size was 35, and this meant that there would be eight students left over. The school board official developed selection criteria to identify the eight children who would be removed from the school.

Imagine, for just a moment, that you are the parent of one of these eight children. You receive a letter in the mail, which states that your child is one of the eight children who were chosen to be removed from the school—the only school that they have ever attended—and you must break the news to your child. Not surprisingly, the children and their parents were devastated. The principal and staff were angry that they had not been consulted. Moreover, the fact that children could be removed from the school set a terrible precedent and could very easily lower future enrolment at the school.

What was most surprising was the reaction of their fellow classmates. They were livid. For many, this was the most unfair thing that they had had to deal with in their young lives.

A meeting was scheduled with school, parents and the newly appointed superintendent of schools. Although the issue of removing the eight children from the school had been decided before the new superintendent had been appointed, he came to the meeting to defend the decision.

Five hundred parents showed up and it was not difficult to detect the anger and hostility in the room. The superintendent made a choice to use humour to defuse the anger and tension in the room. The superintendent said that he could only stay at the meeting for an hour because the movers were unpacking his furniture as he spoke and he didn't want them running off with the silverware.

In this particular case, the superintendent's use of humour had the opposite effect from his intentions. Instead of lowering the tension in the room, it increased it. In terms of context, he was comparing the children's feelings about being removed from their school with the value of his silverware. Secondly, he came off as being insensitive, as his remarks could have been construed as an insult to anyone in the room who was in the moving business or had relatives who were.

The parents then asked if he would rescind the decision. He said, "No." He was asked if the school board had communicated with the school about their decision. He said, "No." He was then asked if any other alternatives were examined, and he again said, "No." He then stated that the process "stunk" and would never be repeated again, but that the decision still stood.

Let's examine what took place in terms of our three-part model. There was a poor substantive outcome—eight children would be removed from the school. The relationship between the new superintendent and the staff and parents at the school was severely damaged to say the least. Finally, all parties agreed that the process used was at best flawed and at worst untenable.

Finally, the meeting ended with the new superintendent agreeing to meet with the parents of the eight children. The school principal and selected staff were asked to attend as well to represent the interests of the school. Under these circumstances a meeting was scheduled. In half an hour, all parties agreed that the eight children would stay in the school. They would be part of a Grade 5/6 split class with a superb Grade 5 teacher who was well-known for her organizational skills. Under the terms of this agreement, the interests of the children, parents, school staff and school board were all well satisfied. The children remained in their school and the school board saved money from a teaching position.

This negotiating process resulted in both a good substantive agreement that well satisfied the interests of all of the parties involved, and a better working relationship between the new superintendent and the school.

In summary, each of the legs of the stool affects the other legs of the stool. Therefore, we must pay attention to all three issues simultaneously: substantive outcome, relationships and process. In addition, a negotiation is made up of a series of choice points.

Choice Points

A choice point is an incredibly important point in the negotiation process whereby, if the negotiator makes a wise decision, the negotiation will move towards an effective resolution. If the negotiator makes an unwise decision, the negotiation will stalemate, break off or tensions will escalate. The example of how the superintendent misused humour in the above example illustrates a poor decision at a choice point. On the other hand, agreeing to meet with the parents and school staff to brainstorm creative solutions illustrates an excellent decision at a choice point.

I would like to give one more example, this time of how humour was used effectively to defuse the tensions in a room. Joe Clark was speaking at a hotel in Sydney, Nova Scotia to garner support for the Meech Lake Accord. I was teaching that morning in a smaller room opposite the one where Joe was speaking. I had enough time to hear his address as his session started before mine did.

As Joe walked up to the platform he was greeted by a loud and derisive chorus of boos, the likes of which I had never heard before. The economy in

Cape Breton was in bad shape, and the people of Cape Breton have an incredibly strong Celtic culture, which they consider equally as distinct as the Quebec culture.

I stood transfixed wondering what Joe would do. He surprised us all by smiling broadly and, in a deep, very warm and friendly tone of voice, saying, "And a hundred thousand welcomes to you, too." Now, Cape Bretoners are known for their love of politics and for their well-developed sense of humour; everyone in the room broke up. Joe had disarmed the entire audience.

Choice points are incredibly important in any and all negotiations. Master Negotiators can identify when they are at a choice point and they have the skills and expertise necessary to make wise rather than unwise decisions. In the above example, Joe Clark disarmed the audience because he knew his counterparts had both a love of politics and a keen sense of humour. If he had been less prepared, and if he had not recognized the choice point and the importance of relationships and the negotiating process, the outcome would not have been nearly as positive, and a civil discussion would not have taken place.

Lloyd Axworthy was Canada's foreign affairs minister from 1996 to 2000. Axworthy is a master at recognizing choice points and changing the negotiation process in order to bring about agreements. Perhaps the highlight of Axworthy's career was the 1997 Ottawa Convention on Banning Landmines.[2] Since that treaty came into force on March 1, 1999, 22 million stockpiled landmines have been destroyed, the number of known producing countries has dropped from 55 to 16 and the export of landmines has essentially stopped.

B.M. *No one seriously believed that any progress could be made on this issue. How did you do it?*

L.A. We helped develop new forms of diplomacy. What we did as Canadians that really made the difference was to broker a broad-based international campaign that was made up of hundreds of organizations such as the Vietnam Veterans of America Foundation, the International Red Cross, like-minded countries such as the Netherlands, Belgium, Norway and NGOs [non-governmental organizations]. It became a grassroots movement of countries and organizations that wanted to put a ban on the export of landmines. A meeting was set in Ottawa in 1996. As well, there were a number of observer nations in attendance such as Russia and the United States.

The meeting was very intensive. I was scheduled to close the meeting on Saturday morning, and we had made absolutely no progress. Large military powers such as Russia, the United States, China, India and Pakistan had no intention of signing the treaty. We also knew that if we went the traditional route though the United Nations Conference on Disarmament, the treaty would be vetoed.

On Friday night I gathered my staff. We all agreed that we had hit a blind alley. The UN Conference on Disarmament was not going to move on this—it would be a dead end.

> *We brainstormed and one of the officials said that if we really wanted to have a way out-of-the-box solution, why not invite everyone back a year from now to sign a landmine treaty outside of the auspices of the United Nations.*
>
> **Lloyd Axworthy**

We brainstormed that Friday night and one of the officials said that if we really wanted to have a way out-of-the-box solution, why not invite everyone back a year from now to sign a landmine treaty outside of the auspices of the United Nations and see how many countries would sign it.

The next morning I invited all of the delegates to come back a year from now and there was a stunned silence. All of a sudden the NGOs and the landmine advocates spontaneously cheered. The level of scepticism from the media and the powerful countries that were against the treaty [was voiced as], "Who did we think we were?"

We rolled the dice. The follow-up was a very intense Canadian full-court press—we worked the diplomatic circuits. I saw officials in the capitals . . . Prime Minister [Jean Chrétien] would raise it, and I became the perpetual nag. We held a series of regional meetings, started drafting a treaty with the help of the Dutch, the Norwegians, the NGOs, part of the new diplomacy coalitions, and partnerships with the like-minded. The treaty was drafted in Oslo. President Clinton took a large lead. The prime minister was on the phone with President Clinton, and I was on the phone with the department of state. We had this incredible mobilization. We metaphorically made the decision to hop off the cliff and asked everyone to come with us.

We applied Canadian diplomacy at its best. We had a high level of skill in our people who were good at negotiating, persuading, communicating, being persistent and drafting. We showed up at every meeting asking why they were not signing this. We used increasing degrees of intensity, the full resources of parliament, the IPU (International Parliamentary Union). Every time they turned around, we were there pushing the agenda of banning landmines and of landmine decommissioning.

B.M. *How did you overcome the many obstacles?*

L.A. It took an extremely high degree of organization and commitment on behalf of the federal government. The civil servants at foreign affairs worked at 150 percent capacity. Everyone knew we had a significant chance to make a positive difference.

B.M. *How did you use strategic alliances to further your cause?*

L.A. One thing that was an element in our favour was the ability of the coalitions to mobilize and come together in a common cause in organizations and in countries throughout the world. Famous people like Princess Diana and Paul McCartney championed this cause. All together, everyone involved put the heat on the parliamentarians in their respective countries.

This interview illustrates the necessity of recognizing choice points, or coming up with creative solutions and using determination, persistence and commitment to bring their vision of a safer and more humane world to fruition. It also demonstrates the necessity of building strategic alliances to develop a critical mass of interested parties to overcome all of the obstacles that would make the difference between critical success and abject failure. We will go into greater detail on the importance of developing strategic alliances in Strategy 6.

In addition to identifying and capitalizing on choice points, Master Negotiators also understand that successful negotiating is a result of how the involved parties relate to one another, the outcome that they aspire to and achieve, and the process by which they get there. To ensure that the negotiation process is successful, Master Negotiators must also understand the following three stages of the negotiating process and know how to complete the required tasks of each stage.

Three Stages of the Negotiation Process

Zartman and Berman's 1982 book, *The Practical Negotiator*, is a classic in the field of negotiations. They define negotiations as "a process in which divergent values are combined into an agreed decision, and it is based on the idea that there are appropriate stages, sequences, behaviours, and tactics that can be identified and used to improve the conduct of negotiations and better the chances of success" (pp. 1-2). Master Negotiators have an intuitive understanding of these stages and the sense of timing required to complete the work of each stage before going on to the next. By better understanding these stages, you will better master the negotiating process.

Zartman and Berman define the three stages of negotiation as:

1. Bringing about negotiation: the diagnostic phase.
2. Defining solutions: the formula phase.
3. Working out agreements: the detail phase.

THE DIAGNOSTIC PHASE

In the diagnostic phase, the participants must listen carefully to each other's stories, and to the issues and interests that are behind those stories. They must decide that negotiation is the preferred method to best meet their needs, and that there is enough trust, common ground and good will/good faith to enter into negotiations.

Alternatively, the participants to a negotiation may decide that the transaction costs of being in negotiation are less than the costs of not negotiating. Transaction costs are the time, effort and sweat equity that one invests in the negotiation. Transaction costs are always part of the negotiation equation and must be factored into one's decision to negotiate. The costs of not negotiating could be the public relations' costs of appearing to be intransigent, or the parties may be in a mutually harmful stalemate, the continuation of which is prohibitive. For example, neither party is winning, nor is likely to, and/or the costs of not negotiating are higher than the costs of negotiating. To put these ideas in context, consider divorcing parents who find that the cost of slugging it out in court and of lawyers' fees for every letter sent becomes so costly to both parties that they become willing to settle their differences through the process of negotiation and/or mediation. Likewise, for many civil litigation cases, the cost of continuing to fight and keeping one's life on hold becomes untenable for all of the parties. The parties enter a mutually harmful stalemate and the process of negotiation is much more likely to take place.

THE FORMULA PHASE

When I read about Zartman and Berman's formula phase, it was as if a light came on in my head. Developing agreed-upon formulas frequently accelerates the negotiation process. Thinking back, developing formulas was something that I did intuitively. Master Negotiators are conscious of this most important element of the negotiation process.

Although there are three basic types of negotiation: inductive, deductive and mixed, most negotiations are mixed. Inductive means that the negotiators start with the small stuff and work up, that is, they work out the issues and details of the negotiation one-by-one until a settlement is reached. Deductive means that the negotiators start with an agreed-upon formula and/or principles, and it is only after the formula and agreement in principle are worked out that the parties work on the details. Mixed is where both processes are used simultaneously. Almost all negotiations are mixed.

A good negotiator comes to the table with several possible formulas and is flexible in changing his or her formulas and in looking at and adapting the formulas or some of the aspects of the formulas proposed from the other side. It is also noteworthy that formulas must be flexible so that they can be changed and/or improved as circumstances change over time. Lastly, no one likes to have formulas—no matter *how* good—imposed upon them. A formula imposed becomes a formula opposed. At this point, I would like to present several examples that demonstrate how powerful Zartman and Berman's idea of formulas is.

One of the shocks of being divorced and having children is that the divorced parents find, usually to their dismay, that they have to negotiate much more after the divorce than they ever had to do when they were married. One of the first negotiations these parents have to tackle is who has the children when. Some of these negotiations are very easy. The husband has the children on his birthday, and the wife has them on her birthday.

Other negotiations are more complex and take more effort and more time to resolve. My ex-wife and I started out with two-day rotations. This worked at first because we were both used to seeing the children every day and enjoyed being actively involved in their lives. On the other hand, it was disruptive to change every two days. The children just got used to being with one parent and then they had to change. It also meant that there were often times when they were in one house and the things that they needed were in another. We then changed to a three-day schedule with my having the children Sunday, Monday and Tuesday nights, my ex-wife having the children Wednesday, Thursday and Friday nights, with Saturday nights negotiable, depending on what worked out best for everyone's schedule. There is flexibility built into the system, but the three-day rotations work extremely well for us. Once we arrived at this basic formula, things got to be much easier for everyone.

The next major negotiation was for the contentious issue of summer holidays. We came to an agreement that we would have first choice of summer vacation dates on alternating years. The next major negotiation after that was for Christmas and Easter holidays. We eventually worked out formulas that were mutually satisfactory for those times as well.

Master Negotiators are aware of how important the development of mutually agreed upon formulas is. Once we become aware of how helpful they can be in reaching successful solutions, we can use the idea of developing formulas more consciously and systematically. Zartman and Berman state that finding a formula is ultimately a matter of skill, intuition, experience, and trial and error. The necessity to work out a feasible formula holds true in all types of negotiations, from business to native land claims to international disputes. Exercises 5-1 and 5-2 have been designed to help you develop a better sense of this skill.

THE DETAIL PHASE

Working out the details verifies the efficacy of the formula. If the formula works as it is being applied, it helps the parties trust that the agreement they are working on is in fact a valid agreement. Be warned, however, expect hostility and anger during this stage. There is a big difference between an agreement in principle and actually working out that agreement in detail. You may find that the formula that worked perfectly in the abstract does not work so well in actual practice, and that the formula may have to be modified or scrapped entirely and a new formula developed that better meets the interests of all parties. It is in this third stage that real sacrifices and concessions have to be made. These sacrifices and concessions are much more painful in

EXERCISE 5-1

Identifying Formulas You Have Used

Think back over three successful negotiations you have been in. Briefly describe the situation and write down the formula that was instrumental in helping to resolve the problem or conflict that brought you to the table in the first place.

1. _____

   _____

   _____

   _____

   _____

   _____

2. _____

   _____

   _____

   _____

   _____

   _____

3. _____

   _____

   _____

   _____

   _____

   _____

EXERCISE 5-2

Observing Others' Use of Formulas

Pick out a Master Negotiator, someone that you can observe, and note in the space below how they use the concept of formulas to negotiate more effectively. Write down three observations that can help you negotiate more effectively.

1. _____
   _____
   _____
   _____
   _____

2. _____
   _____
   _____
   _____
   _____

3. _____
   _____
   _____
   _____
   _____

reality than in the abstract. It is perhaps from all of the above points that the old adage, "the devil is in the details" takes its meaning. Zartman and Berman state, "The settlement of details is a formula's only test and can be accomplished only on a trial and error basis. There are times when speedy agreement on a formula is followed by a long and arduous search for agreement on details" (p. 147).

For example, a divorcing husband and wife make an agreement (develop a formula) to split the furniture 50/50, with both parties keeping the furniture that they had before they were married. The development of this formula was relatively easy. The *details* of who actually gets which CD, video, piece of furniture, picture album, kitchen appliance or casserole dish usually is much slower, more complicated and more likely to engender more heated debate and hostility than the devising of the formula. Although most readers will agree with the above statement, it is also true that the process would be much more arduous and difficult without a formula.

All of the Master Negotiators I interviewed stress the importance of developing an excellent negotiation process. Zartman and Berman state that diagnosing the issues and interests of each party and their negotiation goals, reaching agreement on negotiating formulas and working out the details of the agreement are the essential stages of the negotiation process. Working through these stages thoroughly, thoughtfully and consistently will contribute to successful negotiations. In the next section, I will present 12 guidelines to improve the negotiation process.

Twelve Guidelines to Improve the Negotiation Process

1. Agree on ground rules and guidelines.
2. It may take more time than you ever imagined.
3. You cannot be too careful with wording.
4. Identify the true decision-makers and make your case concise.
5. Use collaborative model building.
6. Inject humour into the negotiation process.

7. Improve your flexibility and adaptability as a negotiator.

8. Remember the importance of saving face.

9. Make sure that you have agreement as to the commitment to carrying out the agreement.

10. Use the power of precedent setting.

11. Disarming the unspoken conversation.

12. Meta-negotiation.

GUIDELINE 1: AGREE ON GROUND RULES

Master Negotiators know the importance of having clearly agreed-upon ground rules and guidelines. Usually, the more formal the negotiation process, the more likely that the ground rules and guidelines will be written down and placed on the wall to help remind the participants of their agreements as to the negotiation process. For example, you may want to agree on turning off cell phones and pagers during the session; where and when you will meet; start and stop times; and guidelines about when it would be appropriate to bring in a facilitator.

GUIDELINE 2: IT MAY TAKE MORE TIME THAN YOU IMAGINED

Working out the proper process often takes more time than anyone ever imagined. When I mediate, I often tell the participants that the process is very similar to rescuing "baby Jessica." Two-and-a-half-year-old baby Jessica fell into an abandoned well in her parents' yard in October, 1987. The rescue team stated that they had to go as fast as they could in order to successfully rescue the child, yet at the same time, they could not go too fast because they did not want to cause a cave-in. In the end, baby Jessica was rescued, but it took a great deal longer than most people thought it would. I often tell this story at the beginning of mediations and some negotiations to help prepare the participants for the time that will be needed to successfully complete the mediation and/or negotiation. Sometimes you simply have to go slow to go fast.

This is not to say that you should always expect the negotiation to take more time than you thought it would. Sometimes you want to do just the opposite; that is, let time's pressure work *for* you. Major-General Lewis MacKenzie calls the time that you have to negotiate your "time horizon." Bill Black of Maritime Life calls it your "time card." No matter what terminology we use, all Master Negotiators know the importance of time and how to use it to their advantage in negotiations. Master Negotiators have developed an inherent, innate sense of timing. They know intuitively when to go slow to go fast, and when to go fast to go fast.

GUIDELINE 3: YOU CANNOT BE TOO CAREFUL WITH WORDING

My colleague, Suki Starnes and I once mediated a difficult situation that had occurred among a team of medical specialists. At the time of the mediation, there was also the distinct possibility that legal action would be taken by one of the specialists against another specialist. The atmosphere in the room was very tense, to say the least. During the first session, we spent three hours developing the ground rules. For obvious reasons, the ground rule that caused us the most difficulty was the ground rule surrounding confidentiality. After a great deal of work, the participants agreed on a definition of confidentiality: what was said in the room would remain in the room. In order to be absolutely clear, we also asked the participants if confidentiality meant that the fact that they were in mediation was confidential. We knew that if they could not reach agreement as to whether or not being in the process of mediation was confidential, one participant might assume that what was said in the room was confidential, but that the fact of being in mediation could be talked about, and for another specialist, both the content of the mediation and the fact that they were in mediation was confidential. This example is illustrative of the fact that you cannot be too careful with the wording.

GUIDELINE 4: IDENTIFYING THE TRUE DECISION-MAKERS AND MAKING YOUR CASE CONCISE

Dawna Ring, Q.C., was legal counsel in one of the most interesting and high profile legal cases in Canadian history. The case I am referring to is Dawna's representation of the spouses and children who became secondarily infected with HIV as a result of tainted blood. Over the last nine years, Dawna provided legal counsel to this group before the Krever Inquiry into Canada's blood system, various challenges to the Supreme Court of Canada, compensation and Red Cross CCAA proceedings. She was also part of the national legal team for the Hepatitis C 86-90 Class Action suit and was a member of the initial negotiation team and co-chaired the Disease Modeling and Damages Committee. Like all of the Master Negotiators I interviewed, Dawna Ring recommends coming to the table 200% prepared. Some of her more unique experiences with negotiations have been with government, both in terms of changing legislation and obtaining compensation. With governments, she also learned that you have to identify the true decision-makers, and to synthesize your case to two pages so politicians will read it.

> *One has to determine what factors are important for the key decision-makers within the government.*
>
> **Dawna Ring**

B.M. *Tell me about the importance of identifying the true decision-makers and making your case concise.*

D.R. In addition to the key elements for negotiations, one has to determine what factors are important for the key decision-makers within the government, what issues are currently before the government, what are their goals as a government, and most importantly you want to know who are the key people in Cabinet. In any Cabinet there are a half a dozen members who are the power brokers and the decision-makers. You need to know what influences them and [what] will cause them to make the decision you want. The facts you collect to support your position must be those facts that influence those power brokers within that government at that specific time.

After all of the above is completed, you need to summarize your case into two pages. Politicians will not read more. They are busy and have many people raising issues for them to consider. To get their attention, your initial approach to government needs to be condensed.

It is like being told by the Supreme Court of Canada you have five minutes to make your argument; even the most complicated *Charter* case must be reduced to two pages.

B.M. *I have a favourite expression: "truth is shorter than fiction" so I take it that you are saying that making it concise forces you to be absolutely clear about the essence of your case, and that clarity helps to make your case more persuasive and convincing.*

D.R. Exactly!

You will learn more about Dawna Ring's work and the importance of strategic alliances in Strategy 6 on building strategic alliances.

GUIDELINE 5: USE COLLABORATIVE MODEL BUILDING

There will be times when the parties do not agree on their assumptions, their facts, and/or what the eventual outcome of a negotiation might look like. This often leads to a breakdown of the negotiation process. One creative option to this dilemma is to engage in a process called collaborative model building. In collaborative model building, the parties build a model that will allow them to try out their various assumptions, and the model—often computer generated—allows the parties to see the result of the various assumptions is a more neutral and dispassionate process. In a seminal article on this process, "Mediating Science-Intensive Policy Disputes,"[3] Connie Ozawa and Lawrence Susskind describe three principles that can be used in collaborative model building to help resolving intense disputes.

> . . . intensive disputes frequently revolve around projections of the likely consequences of proposed actions.

• • •

> If the parties to a technical dispute can develop a model that incorporates key assumptions acceptable to all of them, they are more likely to produce a prediction that none can easily dismiss.
>
> • • •
>
> Models can be used to facilitate a settlement as long as the model structure is perceived as neutral with respect to the interests of the parties involved.[4]

As computer programs become increasingly sophisticated, they will be used more and more to help resolve difficult disputes. An example of collaborative model building using advanced computer programs took place during the Dayton Peace Accord to end the war in Bosnia-Herzegovina.[5] One of the principles that the Serbs and the Bosnians had agreed to was the 51–49 formula, whereby the Bosnians would control 51 percent of the country and the Serbs would control 49 percent. Although the formula was easy to agree to in principle, deciding which parcel of land would be Bosnian and which would be Serbian was an extremely difficult matter to negotiate. In his book, *To End A War*, Richard Holbrooke describes how a sophisticated computer program called PowerScene helped the parties reach an historic agreement.

PowerScene allowed the mediators and the disputants to build a model of all of the land under dispute. By changing the parameters in the program, the parties could try out literally thousands of boundaries and access corridors. The collaborative model building was instrumental in helping them to reach a settlement.

The above example clearly illustrates the power of model building, and in particular, computer model building, in helping to settle disputes. As computer simulations become increasingly sophisticated and the cost of high-end computers and computer programs becomes more affordable, the use of computer modeling to help settle disputes will increase, giving negotiators and mediators one more tool to help settle disputes.

GUIDELINE 6: INJECT HUMOUR INTO THE NEGOTIATION PROCESS

One of the things that effective negotiators have to be on guard against is too much conflict—paradoxically, they also have to be on guard against too little conflict. Too little conflict results in a psychological process called groupthink. In groupthink, the group appears to have reached consensus, even though some of the group members have strong reservations. As a result, conflict is avoided and group solidarity appears intact, even though the wrong decision is being made and/or more viable alternatives exist. Two of the most well-known examples of the negative consequences of groupthink are the "Bay of Pigs" invasion of Cuba (October, 1962) and the launching of, and subsequent demise of, the space shuttle Challenger (January 28, 1986). In both of these situations there were a number of people who had strong reservations about the proposed course of action, but who did not voice their reservations because they did not want to go against the presumed group consensus. With hindsight they wished they had.

Humour can act as a tremendous stress reducer as well as an antidote to groupthink. Humour can accomplish this because it allows us to say things that need to be heard, but they can be heard in a half-hearted way without causing hard feelings. Let me give an example. Groupthink is more likely to occur within hierarchical structures. One way humour is used in one section of the Canadian Naval Fleet Operations is that if anyone feels that the group is starting to engage in groupthink, that person makes a reference to "the Borgs taking over."[6] At that point, everyone has a good laugh and is then more able to look at the problem from different perspectives, and subsequently, develop more varied alternatives to the problem.

GUIDELINE 7: IMPROVE YOUR FLEXIBILITY AND ADAPTABILITY

Flexibility and adaptability have already been identified as essential skills of Master Negotiators. One of the Master Negotiators I interviewed was **Kevin**

Hamm, CEO of Pharmasave Atlantic. Kevin said that improving his ability to understand where the other person was coming from was the first step he took in becoming more flexible. Kevin stated that he was greatly influenced by Stephen Covey's book, *The 7 Habits of Highly Effective People,*[7] and in particular by habit five: "Seek first to understand and then to be understood." The way in which Kevin learned to put this principle into operation is instructive for us all.

Kevin first reaches an agreement with the other party about how they will communicate (meta-communication). The agreement is to let the other party with whom he is negotiating speak first, which enables Kevin to better understand why the other party thinks the way that they do. The agreement also includes the provision that the other party has five to 10 minutes of uninterrupted time to fully explain the situation the way he or she sees it. The phrasing Kevin Hamm uses is, "Let me understand clearly where you stand on this issue."

After the other party has fully explained how he or she sees the situation, Kevin asks for a similar amount of uninterrupted time to fully explain how he sees the situation. Kevin also states that after he has presented his point of view, the other party can contest, challenge, sign on or do whatever he or she needs to do so that they feel fully understood.

Kevin further stated, "In the past, I would not have done this nearly as well. I would get halfway though my sentence, and the missiles would start coming. By giving the other party uninterrupted time, and asking for uninterrupted time on my part, the missiles stopped. At the same time, I now come across as being more fair and as being more of a gentleman."

I have used Kevin's method to become more flexible in my negotiation with my children. For example, when my son Andrew turned 13, I asked him what he wanted for his birthday. He said that he really wanted a portable CD player. My first response was to say "No!" The image that flashed though my head was of my young teenage son walking to school grooving to his music, walking into the middle of traffic and being hit by a car.

I then questioned him as to whether or not he had asked his mother. He had. Her answer was no. But instead of saying no immediately, which is what

I wanted to do, I instead asked him to give me 10 reasons why he should have a portable CD player. His first response was that I wouldn't have to listen to his music, which was a very persuasive statement. He went on to say he could also listen to music while doing chores, which might make him a bit more cooperative when he was asked to do something. His music would not interfere with other members of the family when they were listening to music, and there would be more peace and quiet in the house. After listening to Andrew's reasons, I shared with him my concerns about his safety and the fact that it could easily be stolen. We then came up with a solution (formula) that satisfied both parties. Andrew would not take the CD player out of the house unless he had explicit permission to do so. For example, he could listen to it while doing yard work, putting clothes on the clothesline, etc. Also, with permission, he could take it in the car or on a plane when we went on a trip. The agreement is working perfectly, both parties got what they wanted. A bonus was that my flexibility teaches my children to be more flexible. Also, by giving Andrew the task of organizing and presenting his thoughts concisely he is learning to express himself better. Lastly, we now have a good mental model that we can refer to in helping us resolve other conflicts of interest effectively in the future. Figure 5-3 can help increase your flexibility.

GUIDELINE 8: THE IMPORTANCE OF SAVING FACE

When both sides to a negotiation have become deeply entrenched in their positions, they may become unwilling to compromise. This can make negotiations difficult, if not impossible. Both sides want to remain true to their positions, or to "save face." At this point, coming up with a solution to save face in some aspect of the negotiation is essential to keep it afloat.

Few people have understood the negotiating process as thoroughly as Mahatma Gandhi. The example from India's cotton mill strike in 1918, illustrates the power of allowing all of the parties to save face and the power of creative solutions to satisfy all parties' interests to resolve what was seemingly an intractable problem.

EXERCISE 5-3

Flexibility in Negotiations

In the space below, briefly outline a situation where being more flexible could help you negotiate more effectively. Then list three or four steps that would aid you in this process.

The situation is:

_____

_____

_____

_____

_____

_____

_____

The steps I could take in being more flexible are:

1. _____

_____

2. _____

_____

3. _____

_____

4. _____

_____

For Gandhi, the process or the manner in which the strike was conducted and the manner in which the strikers conducted themselves was as important, if not more important, than the outcome of the strike. However, after a short period of time, things were becoming desperate for the strikers. Many of the workers were starving; they had to sell their furniture and borrow money at high rates of interest. Many lost their homes. Gandhi felt he was in an untenable position. He did not want to compromise the principles, such as decent wages, upon which the strike was based, nor did he wish to see the workers suffer by paying such a high price for their principles.

The labour strike had become very positional. Both sides were dug deeply into their positions and were absolutely unwilling to compromise their positions. The workers were asking for a 35 percent increase. The mill owners had agreed to a 20 percent increase. There seemed no way out of these positions. Gandhi meditated about this situation until he came up with the following suggestion.

> On the first day, an increase of 35 percent will be given in keeping with our pledge; on the second day, we get 20 percent in keeping with the mill owners'. From the third day till the date of the arbitrator's award, an increase of 27 and 1/2 per cent will be paid and subsequently, if the arbitrator decides on 35 percent, the mill owners will give us 7 and 1/2 per cent more, and, if he decides on 20 percent, we will refund 7 and 1/2 percent.[8]

This solution helped both the workers and the mill owners save face. Both sides would be able to be true to their positions, even though it was only for one day. By saving face and being true to their positions, both the workers and the mill owners could be flexible and accept the arbitrator's settlement. Gandhi's proposal also encouraged both the mill owners and the workers to accept the principle of having an arbitrated settlement.

It is important to note that Gandhi looked at the strike as a moment in time; he also knew that his job as leader was to insure good relationships among the workers and between the workers and the mill owners in the future. The ultimate outcome for Gandhi was that "all men are brothers." He now had a powerful, principled way to settle disputes, which worked for positive substantive outcomes and positive relationship outcomes by creating an effective negotiation process.

One of the major differences between this strike and most of the strikes we have witnessed in North America is that one of Gandhi's fundamental principles was that no one should be forced to act against his or her will and/or beliefs, that no one should have to do anything under duress. Therefore, all workers who wanted to work would be guaranteed safe passage to work and they would not be harassed. No worker was forced to behave in any way that was against his or her will, which was guaranteed by Gandhi personally. Gandhi's deep respect for all of the individuals with whom he negotiated was one of the factors that made him such a successful leader, advocate and negotiator. North American management and labour leaders could learn a lot from Gandhi's example.

GUIDELINE 9: GET AGREEMENT AS TO CARRYING OUT THE AGREEMENT

In negotiating with my children, I often thought that I had a clear understanding of and commitment to our negotiated agreement, when in fact the message had not registered with my children. My friend and colleague Master Negotiator Bill Frank has a formula that helps clarify our understanding of what the precise agreement is with our children. The formula is to repeat the agreement three times with three different points of emphasis: "Do you understand?" "Do you agree?" and "Are you committed?" By the time you have gone through this three times, each time asking for understanding, agreement and commitment, they often get it. Conversely, if they agree and understand, but are not committed, it is better to bring this issue out into the open, find out their reservations—which may in fact be valid—and process it, rather than assume you have agreement, understanding and commitment, only to find out later that you did not.

The other classic technique is to ask the other party to summarize his or her understanding of the agreement and/or to get the agreement in writing.

GUIDELINE 10: USE THE POWER OF PRECEDENT SETTING

Master Negotiators know the power of precedent setting and are willing to work long hours to establish a precedent that works well, not only today, but also tomorrow, as the following excerpt from my interview with Lloyd Axworthy point out.

B.M. *Did the Ottawa Convention establish a precedent?*

L.A. Yes, the treaty was not only critically important in and of itself; it was also a precedent that helped establish the human security agenda. It created a reception to establishing new humanitarian laws and standards for protecting an individual's right to the security of individuals such as the International Criminal Court, developing a convention on small arms and developing relief efforts for war-affected children.

> *The treaty banning landmines also gave Canada the confidence that we could be a world-class leader in areas of establishing norms and standards for protecting an individual's right to security.*
>
> **Lloyd Axworthy**

The treaty banning landmines also gave Canada the confidence that we could be a world-class leader in areas of establishing norms and standards for protecting an individual's right to security. Canada could be a tipping agent to help create the critical mass of like-minded countries and organisations to make a . . . difference in how countries around the world treat individual rights.

In December, 2000, Lloyd Axworthy received the first Patrick J. Leahy Humanitarian Award for his role in the treaty banning landmines. This award "recognizes individuals who, through a lifetime of leadership, have dedicated themselves to providing assistance to innocent civilian victims of war and who, though their actions, have expanded and promoted reconciliation, rehabilitation and reconstruction of war-torn people and societies." Canada has an incredibly strong history in peacekeeping and peace making. Lloyd Axworthy—and indeed all Canadians—has every reason to feel proud of this accomplishment.[9] The landmine treaty provided the precedent and leverage needed to establish new, related agreements and negotiations. It also identified Canada as a leader in this area and as a country that would stand behind similar activities.

Master Negotiators never underestimate the power of precedent setting as the following personal story points out. In November, 1991, my family was shopping for shoes at a major Canadian department store. Our 18-month-old daughter Katie was attracted to a display of character slippers, which to her looked like stuffed animals. The character slippers were suspended on pegboard display hooks, one-quarter inch in diameter and eight inches long. She ran over to play with the slippers and unfortunately tripped and fell face first into the display. One of the hooks caught Katie in the eye. We rushed Katie to emergency at the hospital.

The examination showed that Katie's eye had been scratched but miraculously the scratch had stopped one millimetre short of the cornea. We appeared to have been very lucky. However, when the swelling went down and the eye patch came off, we found out that we were not so lucky. Katie frequently fell down, had started holding her head to the right and could not pick objects up off the floor. We went back to the hospital, and after further examination, we were told that there had been some neurological and/or muscular damage caused by the hook pushing the eye back into the orbit. The injury resulted in double vision. Gratefully, Katie's eye corrected itself perfectly within one year.

The accident could have been far more serious and it need not have happened. There had been previous accidents of this type and in fact, much worse accidents have occurred. Ninety percent of accidents are predictable and preventable. I subsequently started a campaign to alert all stores in Canada to the danger of this type of display hook and asked them to be leaders regarding the safety of their customers, especially the safety of children who are the most vulnerable. I made use of the CBC and other various media—television, radio and newspaper—to help put the pressure on retailers to remove the hooks.

I have brought the potential hazard of this type of display hook to the attention of a number of stores. Some, like Chapters, changed their displays immediately. Others have been much more difficult to persuade. Sony Canada, however, deserves a great deal of credit. After notifying Sony of the dangers of single pronged display hooks, I received a letter from them stating that they not only removed all of their single pronged display hooks and replaced them with safer double pronged hooks, they also destroyed all of their single pronged hooks so they could not be used by anyone else in the future. The letter from Sony also stated that they would make a donation of $500 to the Canadian National Institute for the Blind to thank me for bringing this matter to their attention.

The precedent that Sony set, that is, by setting a higher standard than I had even asked for, made it much more likely that other stores would follow suit. For example, the letter from Sony helped me convince the Gap to change all of their display hooks worldwide. In short, the letter from Sony sets a new standard in corporate responsibility. I could use the Sony Canada precedent as leverage in contacting and negotiating with other organizations and as a result of these efforts over 10 million blinding display hooks in Canada have been modified and/or replaced with safer hooks.

GUIDELINE 11: DISARMING THE UNSPOKEN CONVERSATION

An unspoken conversation addresses the things that are known by both parties, but that remain unacknowledged and not verbalized by both of them. When either party addresses the issues that were previously unspoken, it allows the conversation and/or the negotiation to move forward.

I first heard the term unspoken conversation when I had the pleasure of hearing Les Brown,[10] one of the world's most accomplished speakers at the National Speakers Association annual meeting in Washington D.C. in August, 2000. During his presentation, Les introduced the concept of the unspoken conversation. To illustrate this concept, he said that he had written a book about how to make your life work for you—including relationships and marriages. The potential problem was that Les Brown was recently divorced. He acknowledged his divorce in one of the most humorous routines I have ever heard. He talked about meeting a woman at the airport who came up to him and said, "You are Les Brown, aren't you." He said, "Yes I am." She said, "Your book not only turned my career around; it also saved my marriage." Les said, "What page saved your marriage, I want to go home and read it myself." Thus the unspoken conversation that people in the audience might have been having with themselves or their neighbour, about how the master motivator could have had a failed marriage, was clearly acknowledged.

The techniques of surfacing the unspoken conversation and disarming can be combined as the following story illustrates. Tim, aged 30, is a vice president at a major international manufacturing company. The problem was that he looked at least five years younger than his 30 years. This caused problems because the people Tim had to interact with initially had trouble taking him seriously. Therefore, when meeting with high-powered executives from other organizations for the first time, Tim developed a surefire way of surfacing the unspoken conversation about his age.

Tim began the conversation saying, "My company promotes on the basis of merit, and even though I might look too young for the title, the authority and the responsibility that it engenders, I assure you that that is not the case. If you are not convinced that we should be interacting after five minutes of conversation; I will gladly leave and send in someone else." Tim told me that he has never been asked to leave. His strategy of surfacing the unspoken conversation and asking for five minutes of conversation gives him the opportunity to demonstrate his competence and his business acumen and to disarm any negative stereotyping all in one fell swoop.

GUIDELINE 12: META-NEGOTIATION

The prefix "meta" means about. Therefore, meta-negotiation means negotiating to change the type of and/or process of the negotiation that we are in.

For example, one type of meta-negotiation would be changing the negotiation game from face-to-face confrontation to side-by-side problem solving. Let's look at a few specific cases. A husband and wife who are divorcing could each hire competitive lawyers to represent them. This could result in an escalation of their conflict, whereby they could end up with a very expensive suboptimal solution. On the other hand, they could see a mediator with the intention of maximizing their resources, minimizing their expenses and developing the best parenting relationship possible for the sake of their children. In summary, a couple that is divorcing will find that from time to time they engage in both cooperative and adversarial bargaining. However, underlying both types of bargaining, they will negotiate the style of negotiation that will pervade their negotiations. Choosing the style and manner of the negotiation that will pervade their negotiations is a meta-negotiation.

Meta-negotiation can take place at any time during the negotiation. At the beginning of the negotiation it can be a negotiation about ground rules and negotiation procedures, during the negotiation it can be a negotiation about using objective criteria, standards of fairness, bringing in a third party mediator, or taking a break to cool off and start again.

It is important to recognize that a meta-negotiation can take place at any point in the negotiation, and as Robert Axelrod points out, the two sides do not even have to like each other or be in direct communication, for a meta-negotiation to take place. Axelrod wrote an insightful book entitled *The Evolution of Cooperation*. The book examines the conditions under which cooperation evolves. One example describes the way in which the English and German troops in World War I cooperated to minimize the number of fatalities for both sides during trench warfare by firing at each other only at predetermined times so that each side could avoid fatalities. In other words, in the midst of a negotiation, or in this case a war, the participants meta-negotiated an agreement whereby they would fight cooperatively rather than as adversaries. This system of mutual cooperation and live-and-let-live worked until the generals on both sides put a stop to it by forcing the troops to take the initiative in attacking each others' lines of defence.

There are many aspects to conducting a successful negotiation process. Master Negotiators keep the substantive outcome, the relationship between the negotiating parties and the process that will best serve the first two elements in mind at all times. Master Negotiators also understand the importance of choice points; the importance of developing wise and workable formulas to help resolve difficult issues, and the care and attention to details; all the while improving their ability to be flexible and to disarm unspoken conversations.

---

[1] Gerald Williams. "Styles and effectiveness in negotiation." In *Negotiation: Strategies for Mutual Gain*. Lavinia Hall (ed.). Newbury Park, California: Sage Publications, at p. 155.

[2] Convention on the Prohibition of the Use, Stockpiling, Production and Transfer of Anti-personnel Mines and on their Destruction.

[3] *Journal of Policy Analysis and Management* (5(1), 1985): 23-40.

[4] Ibid., at pp. 33, 34.

[5] The General Framework Agreement for Peace in Bosnia and Herzegovina. Initialled in Dayton on November 21, 1995, signed in Paris on December 14, 1995.

[6] This is taken from the science fiction television program, *Star Trek: The Next Generation*. The "Borgs," an alien race, operate as a network of beings that share their intelligence in one mind called "The Collective." Borgs work to assimilate all other beings into their network, at which point, all those assimilated lose all individual freedom to act.

[7] *The 7 Habits of Highly Effective People: Powerful Lessons in Personal Change*. New York: Simon & Schuster, 1989.

[8] Erik Erikson, *Gandhi's Truth on the Origins of Militant Nonviolence*. New York: W.W. Norton & Company, Inc., 1969, at p. 359.

[9] Lloyd Axworthy continues his work as the Director of the Liu Centre for the Study of Global Issues at the University of British Columbia in Vancouver.

[10] Les Brown is the recipient of the National Speakers' Association's highest honour: the Council of Peers Award of Excellence (CPAE). In addition, he was selected as one of the World's Top Five Speakers for 1992 by Toastmasters International and is a recipient of the Golden Gavel Award.

STRATEGY 6

Build Strategic Alliances

Golda Meir, Prime Minister of Israel . . . insisted on face-to-face meetings while negotiating with the Arabs. A journalist questioned the need for these meetings; "Even divorces are arranged without personal confrontation," he said. "I'm not interested in a divorce," Mrs. Meir replied. "I'm interested in a marriage."[1]

Cultural anthropologists tell us that different societies are organized around different defining concepts. One of the major organizing constructs is the emphasis that is placed on the individual versus the emphasis that is placed on community. Clearly, North America, and especially the United States, places a great deal of emphasis on the role of the individual. Many eastern countries emphasize the role of the group, team and collective.

In North America, the role of the individual has achieved mythical proportions. However, if we were to look under the surface, most of our important accomplishments are made through teamwork and strategic alliances.

Strategic alliances can be defined as developing a relationship with another individual(s), organization(s), or company(s) to:

1. put pressure on another party or parties to negotiate, such as I did with the CBC and other media to help change dangerous display hooks;
2. enlist other parties to help the negotiations on your behalf, as Ruth Goldbloom did in getting other prominent Canadians to support the fundraising for Pier 21; or
3. help you better identify the interests of the party(s) you will be negotiating with, to develop more creative options to bring to the negotiating table, and/or to develop a stronger BATNA.

The point to remember is that Master Negotiators are Master Networkers. And all of the Master Negotiators I interviewed used their networks superbly, when necessary, to help them come to the negotiating table better prepared, to help them manage the negotiation process more effectively, and/or to overcome seemingly insurmountable obstacles. One individual who fully understands the power of strategic alliances to overcome seemingly insurmountable obstacles is Janet Conners.

Janet Conners: Building Alliances to Overcome Insurmountable Obstacles

Between 1993 and 1999, **Janet Conners** was front and centre in the media as the principal spokesperson for people who had been secondarily infected with HIV. During that time she proved herself to be a woman of extraordinary courage, warmth and compassion. She is also a charismatic and articulate communicator and a true Canadian leader in every sense of the word.

Janet and her husband Randy were two of the first people to raise the issue of compensation for those who were secondarily infected with HIV. Randy, a hemophiliac, became infected with HIV through tainted blood transfusions. He tested positive for HIV in 1986 and Janet later tested positive in

1989. At the time, wives of hemophiliacs were being told they were not at risk. Janet was stunned by the diagnosis. Throughout the interview, I found Janet to be amazingly candid; although we had booked a 30-minute interview, we both lost all sense of time and ended up talking for 90 minutes.

B.M. *How did you get started as an AIDS activist?*

J.C. We didn't even know what we were doing at first, and we definitely did not want to come out publicly—not for ourselves and especially not for our son, Gus. But we did want to bring the issue to the public's attention. So we set up an initial interview with Dan O'Connell with the local CBC news. We were not prepared to use our real names or faces and the CBC agreed to use only our silhouettes and to disguise our voices. It actually took us quite a while to decide to do this as Janet and Randy Conners. We felt that by using ourselves as Janet and Randy it would better educate people that we were just an ordinary family at the end of the street in Dartmouth. The funny thing is that we only planned to go public this one time only—but that is not the way things turned out.

> *No one was fighting for us, and it soon became clear that this was a national issue and that progress could only be made on a larger scale.*
> **Janet Conners**

Approximately 1,000 Canadians received blood that was contaminated with the AIDS virus early in the 1980s. Initially we were trying to get compensation for people in Nova Scotia. About 20 percent of those who were infected had spouses who were infected, as were 30 percent of the children. The most important thing was that no one was fighting for us, and it soon became clear that this was a national issue and that progress could only be made on a larger scale.

It is from her personal experience that Janet developed the passion and compassion that made her into one of Canada's leading AIDS activists from 1993 to 1999. In 1991, Janet and Randy decided that they had to tell their 11-year-old son Gus that they were both HIV positive and that Randy would probably die within two years. After much thought and rehearsal they sat down with their son. The following excerpt from our interview demonstrates the amount of preparation that went into this difficult conversation.

B.M. *How did you go about telling Gus?*

J.C.   We decided not to tell Gus until we had to. We wanted to spare him from this as much as we could. This was one of the most difficult things we ever had to do—to tell Gus that we were both HIV positive. We decided not to tell him until Randy was very sick and had to be hospitalized with pneumonia.

We wanted to do it right without knowing what or even if there was a right way to do it. We decided that 12 minutes was about all the information he or any of us could handle. Twelve minutes turned out to be just the same amount of time it took to make a Kraft pizza dough rise. So we role-played and role-played until we felt we could do it. And as a matter of fact we did it while the pizza dough was rising. It was important to bring some sense of normalcy back into our lives and making pizza was about as normal as anything could be.

Gus's first reaction was why we didn't tell him sooner; then he wanted to know if he was at risk. He wanted to know if Randy would die soon, and Randy had to say yes. We then had to discuss that "soon" meant most likely a couple of years.

Janet said that one of the most touching moments was when Randy apologized for bringing AIDS into their family. "Gus reached across the table, took Randy's hand and said you don't have anything to apologize for."

By 1994 Janet had become one of the most powerful spokespeople—as a result of alliances, negotiating and persistence—for those who had AIDS, and for those who have been secondarily infected with HIV. According to Janet's lawyer, Dawna Ring, Janet used many strategies that one does not think of as negotiating strategies, such as honesty, warmth, humour, empathy, passion and her ability to stay focused and sincere. Janet also gave people the chance to do the right thing before she condemned their actions, and when they did, she acknowledged it in writing. By the time Janet was done there wasn't a person on the street in Nova Scotia who didn't believe that people who were secondarily infected with HIV deserved to be compensated. Janet's first alliance, with the public, helped support and strengthen her resolve that this was an issue that had to be addressed. Convincing the ministers of health was another matter.

B.M. *How did you go about convincing the ministers of health?*

J.C.   When we were doing this we realized that this was not just an accident, that it was not just an unfortunate mistake. There were people who knew that the Canadian blood supply was tainted with HIV, but they did not want to spend the money to correct a problem that would soon have such tragic consequences.

When Randy and I first started to bring this issue to public attention, we were lucky because we didn't really know what we were doing. We just decided to call the Nova Scotia Minister of Health because we felt that the government worked for us. I wasn't political enough to know that we would be pushed off by so many people who hoped that the problem would just go away.

The importance of developing and maintaining strategic alliances quickly became evident to Janet. Master Negotiators know that they have to find others who can help champion their cause. Janet and Randy Conners found three

such people (George Moody, Alan Rock and Dawna Ring) in their long strug-
gle to bring social justice to those, who through no fault of their own, were
infected with HIV by a system that was supposed to protect them.

B.M. *How did you approach the ministers of health?*

J.C. George Moody [minister of health for Nova Scotia between 1990 and
1993] was an exceptional minister of health. We called his office and
got a meeting a week later. He didn't slough us off on other bureau-
crats. He was honest and direct. He didn't want it played out in the
media until he could make a decision. It cost him a lot in terms of
his reputation with his peers across the country. He really put
himself on the line. The other ministers of health agreed to keep
tabling any discussion concerning compensation.

George Moody then said that he would try to get it back on the
agenda. I said that that wasn't good enough. 'Just take a look at
Randy, he has pneumonia and will soon be dead. Randy is trying so
hard to hold on, but he won't last long.' So George Moody broke
rank. He asked for six weeks to get in touch with them and see if he
could broker a deal.

During the negotiations with the federal government, it just
seemed like there was not going to be any movement. I wrote to
every member of parliament and the prime minister, all 268 of
them and signed every one. I felt that I couldn't use the term
"honourable" with the government of the day because [it was]
refusing to give the community groups the funding that was necessary to participate in the hearings. They actually sued the Krever
Commission because Justice Krever wanted to use individual names
in his report. The Red Cross and the government didn't want to be
able to link the names of the people who were responsible for
releasing the tainted blood with their actions.

The only person I use the word "honourable" with now is Alan Rock [federal minister of health] because he directed his staff to meet with us on the issue of spousal compensation. He made a commitment and the process was very slow. When I got word that one of the women in our group died, I crashed a press conference. I then met with Rock and we hammered out the details till 11 o'clock at night. He championed our cause with the other ministers.

Alan Rock took a lot of heat from some of his provincial and federal counterparts, but I have to tell you he behaved with class and elegance . . . he comes very close to being another George Moody. As a result of their efforts, the tide slowly started turning in our favour.

B.M.   *This was a very long and difficult process. Who else did you turn to for help?*

J.C.   I have an excellent relationship with our lawyer Dawna Ring. Dawna Ring was my voice in a place where I could not use my voice, such as at the Supreme Court of Canada. In our working relationship we don't spare each other's feelings. There are times when we would discuss the meaning of one word for 15 minutes. Dawna and I talked every day. Sometimes it was very hard to do this type of work, especially in the spotlight of the media. We would be each other's support: when she had a tough day, I was there for her and when I had a hard day, she was there for me—and the hardest day of all was the day Randy died.

In my contact with Dawna it was absolutely clear how much these two women admired, cared for and respected each other. Both of these women were as articulate as they were dedicated and as dedicated as they were articulate. When Janet received the "Rebels with a Cause" award from the Elizabeth Fry

Society, in her acceptance remarks she gave the award to Dawna Ring. Janet also tells of the strong relationship she had with her husband Randy. As negotiators, they made a great team, she adds: "My most important strategic alliance was with Randy. We were in this together from the beginning. I remember that I almost lost it in a meeting with one of the politicians we were dealing with. I was going to walk out of the meeting when Randy reached under the table and grabbed my hand. He was not about to let me go."

All of the Master Negotiators I interviewed had the ability to develop the strategic alliances that were necessary to bring their visions to fruition. Janet Conners was no exception. Her personal relationships and her ability to create strategic alliances at local and national levels resulted in a critical mass of political and public support that resulted in the rightful compensation of people who were secondarily infected with HIV.

Strategic Alliances are Critical to Business Success

Bill Gates, founder of Microsoft, said that the 1980s were the decade of total quality management, the 1990s were the decade of re-engineering, and the first decade of the present century will be one of velocity and rapid change. In a similar vein, John Kotter, a leading Harvard Business School scholar and one of this century's greatest thinkers on management and leadership, speaks eloquently about the present decade as a time of increasing complexity, growing competition and escalating customer expectations. Therefore, a fundamental question for our times is: How do organizations survive and thrive in times of rapid and complex change, increased competition and rising customer expectations? One way organizations are coping with these issues is through the development of strategic alliances. Below are two examples of strategic alliances in business settings.

Through deregulation, Air Canada, along with most of the world's airlines, found itself in an increasingly competitive environment. As a former senior Air Canada manager put it: "Competition on some routes was extremely intense, yet we needed to offer our customers seamless service." The answer to this seeming paradox was to create one of world's best known and most widely marketed and advertised strategic alliances—Star Alliance. Star Alliance started forming in 1992 when Air Canada joined forces with one of its previous competitors, United Airlines. Today the alliance also includes: Air New Zealand, All Nippon Airways, Ansett Australia, Austrian Airlines, British Midland, Lauda Air, Lufthansa, Mexican Airlines, Scandinavian Airlines System, Singapore Airlines, Thai Airlines, Tyrolean Airlines, and Varig. Through their combined operations, Star Alliance operates a fleet of 2,299 airplanes and reaches over 894 destinations in 129 countries. It allows the airlines to optimize fleet utilization as well as to feed passengers to each other's airlines. Star Alliance also increases customer satisfaction by providing more seamless travel: common air mile rewards that can be obtained and used on each other's airlines; more convenient scheduling, ticketing and luggage handling; more convenient connections and the use of each others' airport lounges.

The former Air Canada manager stated:

> The skills needed to bring about this type of strategic alliance are complex and have to be honed to the deepest of levels: strategic planning; how to share and have all the partners benefit and increase the bottom line; diplomacy; networking; broadband thinking; conceptual skills; an excellent understanding of operations, the markets, finances and fare structures; an intimate knowledge of the business and inter-governmental affairs; a well honed understanding of power, relationships, and tact; and patience.

In 1999, a strategic alliance in the high-tech industry was formed involving Nortel, Microsoft, Hewlett Packard and Intel. The real promise of computers is not computing, but communications. Today, access to the Internet is relatively slow. By the year 2005, that will change and the real competition will be for who can supply the fastest, cheapest, most convenient high-speed

Internet access. The consortium consisting of Nortel fibre optic cables, Microsoft NT software, Hewlett Packard's Internet servers and Intel's chips will be a hard combination to beat. Just think of the capital resources and the brainpower behind this strategic alliance. This consortium has the power to deal with the rapid change, increasing complexity and competition, and high customer expectations. Also, one-stop shopping will make it much easier for customers because these services are bundled and therefore easier to use and to get help when help is required. The utility of strategic alliances cannot be stressed enough. Alliances put more power behind negotiations and decisions can produce unique results. We will now take an in-depth look at five types of strategic alliances that CO-OP Atlantic has made use of.

Strategic Alliances at CO-OP Atlantic

CO-OP Atlantic operates in grocery, general merchandise and agricultural supplies throughout Atlantic Canada.[2] In all three areas, CO-OP found itself facing gruelling competition. To find out how CO-OP uses strategic alliances to compete more effectively, I interviewed **Eric Claus**, general manager and CEO of CO-OP Atlantic.

Eric described five types of strategic alliances he uses at CO-OP Atlantic:

1. Alliances for customer convenience, customer attraction and customer retention.
2. Alliances for achieving critical mass and thusly being eligible for bulk discounts and rebates.
3. Alliances to bring about synergies between CO-OP's operation and the operations of its suppliers.
4. Strategic alliances that will help CO-OP achieve greater efficiencies by eliminating duplication of services
5. Alliances where strategic information, knowledge and expertise are shared.

Alliances for Customer Convenience, Attraction and Retention

B.M. *How has CO-OP Atlantic used strategic alliances to compete in today's marketplace?*

E.C.   One of the key strategic alliances in CO-OP's five-year plan is to grow vertically because in certain areas we do not have all the expertise to establish new businesses and this is one way to get the expertise. For example, we have a strategic alliance with a large pharmacy franchise called Medicine Shoppe Inc. that will help us get into the pharmacy business. . . . This will eliminate one step for our customers because they will be able to do their grocery shopping and shop for prescription and over-the-counter pharmaceuticals in one store. Considering how busy people are, the convenience of one-stop shopping will be a draw for both grocery shoppers and pharmaceutical shoppers.

The strategic alliance between CO-OP and Medicine Shoppe Inc. demonstrates other advantages of cooperation. They will supply us with pharmaceuticals and over-the-counter medication, we will bulk buy for them on our private label direct import program from the Orient. And we will see more of this in the future.

Alliances for Achieving Critical Mass

B.M. *How have strategic alliances helped CO-OP Atlantic to remain competitive in the face of such large and well-funded competitors like Wal-Mart, Sobeys and Loblaws?*

E.C.   It is critical that we achieve size and critical mass. Half the business section of any major newspaper has to do with mergers and acquisitions. In the past year, the food industry in Canada has seen the emergence of two players who control 56 percent of the market share in the grocery business. We belong to a buying group called UGI. To increase our power in that buying group, we are partnering with other co-ops and other businesses to get volume rebates. It is necessary to buy together because size and critical mass dictate the rebates we get. If we do not form these alliances, we will not remain competitive. To that end, the Canadian CO-OP CEO Council meets twice a year to talk about strategic alliances that we can form. The first order of business is to talk about discounts through collective buying. Together, we do $35 billion in business in Canada. We can achieve a critical mass and therefore be eligible for discounts and rebates through our collective buying power.

Alliances to Bring about Synergies between CO-OP and its Suppliers

B.M. *How has CO-OP Atlantic used strategic alliances between itself and its suppliers?*

E.C. The objective of this type of strategic alliance is to have trading partners that will look out for our best interests while we look out for theirs. For example, we have suppliers using new replenishment technology that links directly to our distribution centres and allows them to replenish their item stocks in our distribution centres. We are also partnering with a local meat packer and local farmers. We have a contract to supply the farmers with grain for 10 years, the farmers [sell the] pork that was fed with our grain [to the meat packer], and we buy the pork from the local meat packer for our stores. This is a three-way strategic alliance. We are now working on a similar program to supply, sell and market a more consistent quality of eastern beef to compete more effectively with western beef.

Alliances to Eliminate Duplication of Services

B.M. *Are there other examples where the strategic use of strategic alliances have led to cost saving?*

E.C. We are also looking at strategic alliances to reduce duplication of services. If there are five CO-OP's doing the same thing, there is clearly room for cost savings and that will help us compete with some of the other giants in our industry.

Alliances to Share Information, Knowledge and Expertise

B.M. *This is an impressive list, do you have one last example?*

E.C. How else can we survive and thrive in a world of mergers and acquisitions? We are sharing information with other regional organizations in both Canada, and the U.S. and even overseas. Due to the fact that we are cooperative in nature we are more inclined to share with each other. For example, CWS is the Cooperative Wholesale Society in Great Britain. We shared information with them and they shared their member benefit program with us. This is a program that they spent a great deal of time and money developing. We benefited greatly from their information, knowledge and expertise as they benefited from ours. Therefore, an important, but often overlooked, aspect of strategic alliances is the sharing of information.

> *Due to the fact that we are cooperative in nature we are more inclined to share with each other. We benefited greatly from their information, knowledge and expertise as they benefited from ours.*
> **Eric Claus**

When I asked Eric how much time he spends developing and maintaining strategic alliances, he concluded that approximately 15 percent of his time is spent on strategic alliances. I then asked him how much time he spends thinking about the future of his organization. He told me that most of his time, almost 65 percent, is spent thinking about the future.

B.M.   *What are the essential skills needed to create strategic alliances?*

E.C.   You have to be forward thinking, you have to get past the little things of today, you have to be a visionary and you have to think out-of-the-box. You have to be able to give—and that is tough for a lot of people—you have to be able to bare your soul, open up your books, and you have to know that you are not the best at every-thing. In a strategic alliance, you are giving up functions or tasks that someone else is going to do for you.

You have to be patient because strategic alliances do not happen overnight. At the same time, you have to have the ability to seize the opportunity. You have to jump on it quickly, because if you don't, it will be too late, and someone else will have taken it or it will no longer be there.

You have to have a great ability to communicate with people and to network. Personal charisma will also do you well. Lastly, you have to have both short- and long-term analytic ability, and a good understanding of the numbers.

> *You have to be patient because strategic alliances do not happen overnight. At the same time, you have to have the ability to seize the opportunity.*
> **Eric Claus**

The skills described by Eric Claus take a lot of time and experience to develop. Wise companies would be well advised to select CEOs who have the skills and abilities necessary to develop and negotiate powerful strategic alliances and who can train others in their companies to do the same.

Although Eric Claus talked about five important areas where strategic alliances are being developed, he made it clear that one has to continually think outside the box if one's company is going to survive and thrive. To help make his point, he gave one last example of that type of outside-the-box think-ing. "We may even see strategic alliances between competitors, for example, we might share a distribution centre because it makes sense to both of us."

Once I began exploring the area of strategic alliances, I started seeing them everywhere—Wendy's and Tim Horton's, Harvey's and the Second Cup, just to name a few, and each of these strategic alliances have to be negotiat-ed. It is not unlike buying a Honda and then being surprised at how many Hondas one sees on the road. Clearly, developing strategic alliances and the skills necessary to bring them about will be one of the most important skill sets of the twenty-first century. These are skills that everyone should learn about and master to the greatest degree possible.

I am encouraged by the number of team projects that my children have to work on in school compared to my own school memories where almost all of the projects were individual ones. In sum, all of the interviews I have had with Master Negotiators emphasize the importance of learning how to nego-tiate strategic alliances. Our individual prosperity, the prosperity of our organizations and our collective standard of living depends on our ability to negotiate strategic alliances.

STRATEGIC ALLIANCES AT MARITIME LIFE, HOME DEPOT CANADA AND PIER 21

Strategic alliances are about creating value and developing synergies that would not take place without the strategic alliance. All of the Master Negotiators I spoke with expressed the importance of strategic agreements and alliances in the process of negotiating.

During our interview, Bill Black, president and CEO of Maritime Life Assurance stated:

> On both the asset management side and on the distribution side, strategic alliances and strategic agreements are what make our busi-ness. Our ideal of an alliance is for *decades*—we don't even think in terms of a year or two—we invest a lot in the early years.

It is because of Maritime Life's commitment to strategic alliances at all levels that the philosophy at Maritime Life is to treat all acquisitions, including the acquisition of Aetna, as a merger because that is the best way to grow the business, to grow the people and to grow the culture. It will take more time, and more effort in the short run, but it is definitely worth it in the long run.

Annette Verschuren, President of Home Depot Canada concurs:

Strategic alliances are really critical to everything from the vendors who support us, the Canadian manufacturing industry, the carriers, the logistics systems suppliers, to the installers that work with us. Our ability to negotiate strong alliances across key areas is absolutely critical to our success.

I am a big believer in establishing long-term goals and short-term results. Our key objective in executing strategic alliances is to have more products flying though our doors and theirs.

The personal business relationships that we develop with the key vendors who work with us are very critical. For example, we started with 19 stores in 1996; we will have 78 stores by the end of 2001. Each store costs from $10 to $15 million to construct. So you can imagine the investment we are putting out there in the construction industry. And we are working to make our strategic alliances work better and better, that is, with legal firms, architectural firms or the construction companies we work with. I call the people we work with through our strategic alliances our invisible aprons. That may make more sense when you know that the apron is a sign of service to Home Depot.

Another master at strategic alliances is Ruth Goldbloom. In fact, it was through Ruth's network of strategic alliances that $9 million was raised to bring the Pier 21 project to fruition. At the end of our interview, I asked Ruth for leads of other Master Negotiators whom I should interview. Ruth brought out her old black address book and gave me the names and telephone numbers of several extremely good contacts. I must admit that I was struck by the fact that even though my own computerized contact management system is infinitely more sophisticated than Ruth's old-fashioned black book, there was absolutely no question as to whose system had the more powerful contacts.

Just as Bill Black, Annette Verschuren and Ruth Goldbloom are masters at building strategic alliances, so were each and every one of the Master Negotiators I interviewed. Frank McKenna built a strategic alliance with NBTel and CO-OP Atlantic to bring more jobs to New Brunswick, Frank King built strategic alliances to bring the XVth Winter Olympic Games to Calgary, Major-General Lewis MacKenzie built at least a partial strategic alliance among the warring factions in the Bosnian civil war to re-open the Sarajevo Airport and Paul Tellier built strategic alliances with the management and unionized workers at the Canadian National Railway to turn a failing organization into one of North America's more effective and efficient railroads. Paul Tellier also formed a strategic alliance with CN's former nemesis, the Canadian Pacific Railroad, to share track and the maintenance thereof in western Canada that will bring $30 million a year in savings to both railroads. That is $30 million a year that can be invested more effectively in their respective futures.

Strategic alliances do not grow in a vacuum. Exercise 6-1 will help you access your strengths in building strategic alliances and identify areas for future growth.

Individuals, teams and organizations working together synergistically are responsible for most accomplishments. In interview after interview, for my previous books, for this book, and for different articles that I write and publish in the *Negotiation Newsletter*, the Master Negotiators that I interviewed were clear on the importance of developing the ability to negotiate strategic alliances.

Master Negotiators also know that no matter how well they have developed their skills, it is imperative to keep learning. Therefore, in Strategy 7 we will turn our attention to becoming a life-long learner.

---

[1] *The Little, Brown Book of Anecdotes*. Boston: Little, Brown, 1985, at p. 394.

[2] Atlantic Canada refers to Nova Scotia, New Brunswick, Prince Edward Island, and Newfoundland and Labrador where as the Maritime provinces refers to all of the above except Newfoundland and Labrador.

EXERCISE 6-1

Strategic Alliances Worksheet

In the space below list three of your most important current strategic alliances.

1. _____

2. _____

3. _____

In the space below, list three current strategic alliances that you could develop further.

1. _____

2. _____

3. _____

In the space below list three potential strategic alliances that would be worth future exploration.

1. _____

2. _____

3. _____

STRATEGY 7

Become a Life-Long Learner

I learned, as chairperson of the school board, as much about negotiating, influencing, mediating, consensus building, media relations and how to get one's message across as I could have in two master's degree programs. The learning curve was steep and intense and I loved every minute of it.

Stella Campbell, former chairperson, Halifax Regional School Board

In addition to using the six strategies already discussed, the Master Negotiators that I interviewed were all dedicated life-long learners. In fact, it is their dedication to life-long learning that helps them become Master Negotiators in the first place. We can define life-long learner as someone who has the passion and dedication to learn from every source available. It doesn't matter if that source is their own personal experience, learning through the experience of others, or learning from their own personal failures and hardships.

Strategy 7 covers five critical areas that are necessary to become life-long learners:

1. Obtain salient feedback.
2. Learn from coaches, mentors and mastermind groups.
3. Learn how to think like the experts.
4. Interview the best negotiators and influencers you can find.
5. Learn from the best books, movies and courses.

Strategy 7 also includes action plans to help you fully develop the strategy of becoming a dedicated life-long learner.

Lessons of Experience: How Master Negotiators Learn Their Skills

The Lessons of Experience: How Successful Executives Develop on the Job by McCall, Lombardo and Morrison is one of the most important business books that was written in the last 25 years.[1] This book was based on groundbreaking research at the Center of Creative Leadership, in Greensboro, North Carolina in which the authors investigated how managers, executives and leaders learn. What makes this book particularly interesting is that the authors were able to quantify the sources of learning. The authors demonstrate that 50 percent of what executives learn is learned from experience. The authors call this "trial by fire" which means "job challenge and specifically difficult assignments are indeed the best teachers" and "[t]he essence of development is that diversity and adversity beat repetition every time."

Twenty percent of what managers and executives learn is learned from good, bad and flawed bosses. From the good bosses one can learn what to do, from the bad bosses one can learn what not to do, and from the flawed bosses one can learn that everyone has weaknesses or flaws. If one does not keep his or her weaknesses and flaws under control, they will lead to one's downfall.

Twenty percent of what an individual learns is learned from failure and hardship. For example, I can learn more from teaching a course that doesn't go well than I can learn from over 100 courses that were very successful. Failure can be a hard, but necessary lesson.

The last 10 percent of what is learned stems from formal education. Although this only accounts for 10 percent, it can be an incredibly important 10 percent if the education relates to the overall learning goals and objectives of the individual in question, and if the learning occurs at the right time.

I interviewed Master Negotiator Stella Campbell to find out how she learned her negotiating and influencing skills. The following interview documents the difficult tasks that Stella faced, first as a member of and then as chairperson of the Halifax Regional School Board. In the second half of the interview, Stella articulates seven ground rules that she developed based on her experience.

It is interesting to note that all the Master Negotiators I interviewed placed themselves in situations where they accelerated their learning of the Seven Strategies of Master Negotiators. Whether through learning gleaned on the job, from mentors, both positive and negative, or from experiencing failure or difficulties, these Master Negotiators brought McCall, Lombardo and Morrison's findings to life.

Stella Campbell and the School Board

Stella Campbell was first elected to the Halifax Regional School Board (HRSB) in 1994. She served as a board member for four years and was elected chairperson for the last two years of her tenure. It should be noted that Stella was on the HRSB and served as its chair during one of the most difficult time in HRSB's history.

There are four primary reasons why these were difficult times for the board. The first was that provincial funding for education in Nova Scotia was the lowest out of all the Canadian provinces. Therefore, by almost any standard, education had been and still is under-funded in the province. Secondly, the newly elected government of Premier John Hamm had a mandate to reduce the provincial debt. Because the debt and the payments to service the debt were so high, the Hamm government's alternative was to drastically reduce spending, and this included reduced spending to an already under-funded educational system. Thirdly, the three former school boards had a long tradition of running the school in their respective areas. All of this changed with their amalgamation into one unified board in 1996. If all of the above were not enough to make the task of integrating and running the new HRSB difficult, there was one more issue that was particularly divisive: the issue of supplementary funding. The municipalities of Halifax and Dartmouth had, for the previous 20 years, elected to pay higher property taxes in order to help insure that they had a higher standard of education than they would have had if they had not voted for supplementary funding. Bedford and Halifax County did not have, and did not want to have supplementary funding. They preferred to vote in extra money on an as needed case-by-case basis. The net result was that there was a basic inequality built into the new HRSB.

B.M. *What was your vision for your role as chair of the Halifax Regional School Board?*

S.C. Because of the amalgamation of the three previous school boards [Halifax, Dartmouth, and Bedford and Halifax County] this was not only a time when there was an astonishing amount of work which had to be done, but it was also a time of great opportunity. With the demise of the three former school boards, we had the opportunity to look at virtually everything from a new perspective. The optimists thought we had a chance to bring forward the best programs and traditions from each of the three boards. As well, the new larger board could benefit from the economies of scale and the synergy inherent in the new Halifax Regional School Board. The pessimists, on the other hand, saw the amalgamation of the boards as a loss of local autonomy and a sinking to the lowest common denominator. For example, the former Halifax District School Board had a French immersion program starting at kindergarten. Bedford and Halifax

County had French immersion programs that started in Grade 7. Since the new school board wanted to be fair, that is, to be able to offer the same programs to all of its students, should it then have a full immersion program starting at kindergarten for all of the students clear across the board? And if so, where would the extra money come from? Should they instead start French immersion in Grade 7 all across the board? What about the research that shows that early immersion is more effective and if you wait until Grade 7, a smaller percentage of boys will enrol in French immersion. Or should we do the traditional Canadian compromise and start all of the students in middle immersion in Grade 3?

This is but one example of what the three former school boards had to consider. There were also considerable differences in music and art programs. As well, some schools had serious problems with declining enrolment, while other schools were filled and overflowing. At the same time, the province had been building new state-of-the-art schools replete with the latest computers, data projectors, high-speed Internet access, and smart boards,[2] while other schools were lucky to have any computers at all.

We had to make the new board think of itself as a new board, even though there were strong local interests. I also had to lead them to think of what was best for all of the 58,000 students from elementary school to high school who were under our care.

With the demise of the three former school boards, we had the opportunity to look at virtually everything from a new perspective.

Stella Campbell

In the following interview you will learn how Stella came to the table incredibly well-prepared, used strategic alliances, objective criteria and optimal solutions and managed the negotiation process just like the other Master Negotiators we have met so far. In addition, we will focus on how Master Negotiators turn their experiences into life-long learning.

B.M. *Although you might want each of the school board representatives to think about what was best for all of the 58,000 students the board was responsible for, how could you get them to think this way in reality?*

S.C. We looked at the best practices from each of the former school boards and brought them forward. Each school board was inward looking and had built up many traditions—some of which worked well and some of which did not. The former Halifax District School Board had a tremendous stringed instrument program and was afraid that they would lose it. We brought that forward because the former Halifax District School Board valued strings.

We could forge ahead only if we took a strong leadership role so people could feel part of the new board, and eventually we learned to debate the issues themselves—based on their merits not on which school board they used to belong to.

For example, we developed a strategy to extend supplementary funding throughout the school board over a period of five years. Council debated it four times and voted it down four times. However, it was not a subject that I would let go away. I kept coming back to the other councillors. At times I would deliberately put them in the hot seat as to the difference that supplementary funding would make to the students in the area that they represented. I let them know that they were choosing the level of education that the students in their area would receive. I also let them know that I understood that politically, this was a very sensitive area; that I agreed that the province was not paying its fair share of the education budget and that it could easily be argued that since supplementary funding was based on property taxes, that the property owners would be paying more than their fair share.

I then went back and asked the mayor to put it on the agenda one more time. I told him that I knew that he and the councillors didn't believe that children in one area are more important than another.

I also asked that we have it verified by an external auditor to prove what we get or don't get from supplementary funding. When the report was in we could prove that the class size in Halifax and Dartmouth was smaller than that in Bedford and the County, that we were able to provide more music, art, resource teachers and librarians in Halifax and Dartmouth.[3]

Through Stella's persistence she was successful in getting supplementary funding throughout all of the HRSB. This was a major victory for education.

STELLA CAMPBELL'S SEVEN RULES TO BE AN EFFECTIVE NEGOTIATOR

Based on her experience as a life-long learner, including her experience at the school board, Stella developed the following seven rules to be an effective negotiator:

1. Never take it personally.
2. Listen to multiple points of view.
3. Ask the right types of questions.
4. Insist on using objective criteria.
5. Sometimes small steps can make a big difference.
6. Develop strategic alliances with the media.
7. Never, never give up.

Rule 1: Never Take it Personally

Having attended some very intense meetings at my children's school I was amazed at how passionately parents felt about their children's schools. I have also seen anger and rage directed at both the elected school board members and at the chair. The anger and rage are most intense when the board decides that a community's school has to close.

B.M.   *How do you apply your rule of not taking it personally?*

S.C.   My son was a student in our city's school. When he was in school, I would fight like a tiger to protect his interests, so it is very easy for me to understand that people have strong feelings and I believe that every person has a right to be personally passionate. However, when I am in the role of spending the taxpayers' money, I have an obligation to those taxpayers. If a child's parent has a good reason, I have to be able to write down and articulate that reason or those reasons—feeling passionately is not enough. We only have so much money and we want it to have the most impact. Parents have the right to be the advocate for their child; I have to be an advocate for 58,000 children.

Rule 2: Listen to Multiple Points of View

B.M.   *How did you deal with so many diverse points of view?*

S.C.   I made a strong effort to be in all of the areas and attend more meetings than I can count. My constituents have a fundamental right to be listened to. I didn't always agree with them, but I honoured their right to be heard.

Rule 3: Ask the Right Types of Questions

B.M.   *How important is it to ask the right questions?*

S.C.   The type of question you ask makes all the difference in the world. That is the most important thing in dealing with all of the stakeholders. You also have to be astute enough to recognize code words to be able to understand the true meaning of some of the answers you receive.

Rule 4: Insist on Using Objective Criteria

Throughout the interview, it became very clear to me that one of the reasons that Stella was so effective as a negotiator was her passion for being fair and that fairness had to be based on truth and that truth had to be based on objective criteria.

B.M. *Could you provide a specific example of using objective criteria?*

S.C. The provincial funding for the Halifax Regional School Board was one of the worst funded in the province. In fact, the HRSB was not getting its fair share of the funding and this was agreed to by the provincial education funding review group, which has representation from all the boards. At the same time, the new government was on a steep learning curve. We knew we had to be as persuasive as possible, so we used the provincial department of education's own statistics to complete a board-by-board funding analysis because it would be hard for the government to argue against its own data. The data proved that the HRSB was underfunded. We then called the media because we had to get this information on the table.

Rule 5: Sometimes Small Steps Can Make a Big Difference

B.M. *Sometimes small steps can change the whole tone and tenor of a negotiation. Can you give me an example?*

S.C. One of the biggest controversies that the school board had to face was an area review of south end Halifax schools. Due to the increase in real estate values more and more families with young children were moving from the south end to the suburbs. As a result we had an excess of schools. A decision was made to close Tower Road Elementary School and move the Tower Road children across the street to St. Francis Elementary School. The Tower Road School had a deeply loyal, articulate and committed parent teacher association, but it just didn't make economic sense to run two schools, neither of which were full, when all of the students could be accommodated in one school.

Knowing how the two schools would be integrated would be the foundation upon which the "new" school would exist, all of the parties decided that the new school should have a new name, and that the students should choose the new name. As a result, the students decided to call the new school the Inglis Street Elementary School after Inglis Street, which was the street the school was located on. Having the children name the school had an amazing healing effect on the students and parents who had previously been at intense odds.

Rule 6: Develop Strategic Alliances with the Media

B.M.   *The media play a crucial role in how issues are perceived by the public. How did you turn the media into a strategic ally?*

S.C.   I have a greater respect for the media than I ever did before coming onto the school board. I found out that the media wants information that is correct and factual. The one thing that the media won't forgive is incorrect information. I also learned that when I didn't have the information, I had to say so—I always had to be on the level because my credibility and that of the school board was at stake, otherwise the media would lose faith in me and I would lose a valuable ally . . . [in] communicat[ing] effectively with the parents of the 58,000 children who were my constituents. I had to make sure that the information was as accurate as I could make it.

Stella also said that she got better at working with the media as she learned more and more about how they operated and what their needs were. She went on to say:

Initially, I made the mistake of overloading them with information. Then I realized that everyone has been downsized, including the media. They need short clips because that's what works on TV. Rather than complaining about the seven-second clip, I learned to work within their limitations and how to give the most salient information as clearly as possible. I also learnt quickly what didn't work. I used sarcasm one day and it was in the papers the following day—I never used it again.

Rule 7: Never, Never Give Up

B.M. *Sometimes you have to be incredibly persistent to achieve a negotiated agreement. Can you give me an example where persistence paid off?*

> *Rather than complaining about the seven-second clip, I learned to work within their limitations and how to give the most salient information as clearly as possible.*
>
> **Stella Campbell**

S.C. During the time we were negotiating for supplementary funding across the whole board, we went to council four times. We stated that we could not justify a two-tiered educational system in the same board. We were told again and again that it would not be possible to raise taxes and it was voted down. The last time we went to the mayor and asked to put it on the agenda again. It was just prior to a municipal election—not a good time for municipal councillors to raise taxes in their areas—it passed. If the need for change is based on a powerful premise—and in this case it was equity of educational opportunities for all children in the same board—then change will eventually occur.

Stella had announced her intention to leave the school board by not seeking re-election in the elections held in October, 2000, the month our interview took place. This was the perfect time for my next question.

B.M. *What do you see as your legacy to the HRSB?*

S.C. I can tell you . . . that my ultimate goal was to work hard on the school board so we could be a smart province. In order for us to be a smart province, we have to nurture all of our schools. We worked hard at identifying goals for the new superintendent. We absolutely needed better financial information and we now have it. We needed to restructure our system so that people, both within and outside of the system, would know who to call for the specific information they needed. We established area offices so people would know who to call, and time lines about when to get back to them.

What was Stella's legacy? I can tell you that in speaking with her colleagues and constituents, they told me that Stella's view of her accomplishments was much too modest. One of her colleagues expressed it best when he said, "Stella went on the school board because she wanted to make a positive difference in education and make a commitment to the community." During her tenure, she became not only the spokesperson for the school board but also the spokesperson and an advocate for education in the province. Stella, like all of the Master Negotiators I spoke with, embodies one of my favourite quotes by Ann Lee, founder of the Shaker religious sect: "Do all your work as though you had a thousand years to live and as you would if you knew you must die tomorrow." Master Negotiators embody both a strong sense of patience and a strong sense of urgency. We will now turn to techniques that you can use to become a life-long learner.

Five Critical Techniques for Life-Long Learners

TECHNIQUE 1: OBTAIN SALIENT FEEDBACK

Although we live in a feedback-rich world, most of us do not do a good enough job of harvesting the feedback that exists to help us become better negotiators. Examples of how Master Negotiators have successfully learned the process of obtaining salient feedback will be used to illustrate the five techniques necessary to maximize feedback and effectiveness. The six techniques to increase the amount of salient feedback we receive are:

1. the 3 x 3 debriefing form;
2. writing letters asking for feedback from people we have negotiated with;
3. a guaranteed technique for managers and supervisors to receive the feedback they need to receive but didn't know it!;
4. individual, team and organizational surveys;
5. being vigilant in developing methods and opportunities to maximize feedback at work; and
6. seeking feedback from spouses, children and significant others.

The 3 x 3 Debriefing Form

The 3 x 3 debriefing form was designed to help you get more systematic feedback on what you do well as a negotiator in addition to providing targets for improvement. Research has documented the fact that we tend to be poor observers of human behaviour and that we become much more accurate when we have a systematic method of data collection. In addition, we get much more accurate feedback by asking at least three different people to rate us.

There are a number of criteria to consider when choosing the people who will respond to the form. You need to choose someone who is both free to and capable of giving you honest, direct and straightforward feedback.

There are three reasons for starting with positive feedback as to what one does well.

1. It is important to be acknowledged for what we do well—no one in any of my training sessions has admitted that they suffered from too much positive feedback.
2. Behaviour that is acknowledged and reinforced tends to occur more frequently.
3. Positive feedback is often very instrumental in helping us develop the focused motivation necessary to work harder in those areas that we want to improve.

It is a good idea to separate the feedback from work and from home because we may negotiate differently in those settings. Therefore, I recommend that you start in either of these two important settings, but don't mix the two. Lastly, an alternative method of data collection is to ask a neutral third party to collect the data for you and then present you with a summary of the data in such a way that no specific respondent could be recognized. Exercise 7-1 contains a copy of the 3 x 3 debriefing form.

Request Feedback in Writing from People You Have Negotiated With

I had the good fortune of working with the Department of Fisheries and Coast Guard during the raising of the *"Irving Whale"* in 1996. The *"Irving Whale"* was an oil barge that sank off Prince Edward Island in the Gulf of St. Lawrence on September 7, 1970. The barge contained bunker "C" oil that was slowly leaking into the undersea environment.

At a cost of $28 million, the raising of the *"Irving Whale"* was the largest maritime environmental prevention operation in Canada's history. The government was in a seemingly no-win situation. If they did not remove the barge, it could come apart on the ocean floor causing a major oil spill. If it came apart during the salvage, there would also be a major spill, and the salvage opera-

EXERCISE 7-1

3 x 3 Debriefing Form

Name _____

Please list three specific things I do well as a negotiator. For example, "Pat is a good listener" is not specific. "Pat makes good use of high-yield questions, and pauses long enough for the other party to answer" is specific.

1. _____

2. _____

3. _____

Please list three specific targets for improvement. For example, "Terry needs to improve his or her listening" is not specific. "Terry needs to pause after asking high-yield questions to give the other party enough time to answer," is specific.

1. _____

2. _____

3. _____

From *The Seven Strategies of Master Negotiators* by Brad McRae © 2002, McGraw-Hill Ryerson.

tion as a whole and the government would lose a great deal of credibility. Needless to say, the whole operation was under a great deal of media scrutiny.

Not only was the salvage a success, the government also showed a great deal of wisdom in setting up a two-day debriefing session for all parties involved so they could document what had been done well, as well as highlight things they would do differently if faced with a similar situation in the future. I had been selected as one of two outside facilitators whose job was to keep the process focused and on track.

One of the most interesting parts of the debriefing was listening to Susan Martin,[4] who was responsible for negotiating the contract between the government of Canada and the American/Canadian consortium that was responsible for the salvage operation.

After the barge had been successfully raised and the terms of the salvage contract were successfully completed, Susan wrote to the president of the salvage company and asked him for feedback on what she had done well in negotiating and writing the contract on behalf of the government of Canada, and what she could do better if she were to negotiate a similar contract in the future. Susan received a concise one-and-a-half-page letter, outlining the many things she did well, as well as two suggestions for improvement, all of which was extremely valuable feedback. How many people would have gone to the effort to write such a letter? The answer may be one in a thousand. Harvesting salient feedback is used strategically by Master Negotiators. It should be noted that salient feedback is equally as powerful at home as it is at work.

A Guaranteed Technique For Managers and Supervisors to Receive Feedback

What we do not know, but need to know, can hurt us! We have all felt remorseful because we didn't have an important piece of information or we sort of knew something was not quite right but didn't pay enough attention to our intuition. There is a technique that managers, supervisors and leaders use to be more pro-active in receiving the feedback they need to receive. And it is incredibly simple! Every month send out a letter or e-mail and ask your staff the following two questions:

1. What are three things I am doing that help you do your work more effectively?
2. What are three things I am doing that get in the way of your doing the work as effectively as possible?"

As an example, Kevin Hamm CEO of Pharmasave Atlantic used this technique. The last time he used it, Kevin received the following feedback.

Three of the things that I was told I did well were:
1. Motivating the troops.
2. Seeing our potential and promoting from within.
3. You give me total control of my department and let me learn from my mistakes.

The three targets for improvement were:
1. Listen more effectively; sometimes I feel that I don't have your full attention.
2. Spend more time with each department.
3. Spend more time with us, particularly in one-on-one coaching.

Warning! Not everyone can use this technique. Some people who say they are open to constructive feedback really are not. They will, subtly, and in some cases, not so subtly, punish those who took them at their word and provided honest feedback. The damage that this can do to your credibility will often cause irreparable damage. An alternative is to have this information collected by a neutral third party from either inside or outside the organization. An example of a Manager/Leadership Evaluation Form that we developed at McRae and Associates can be found at Figure 7-1. The following has been found to be particularly effective in generating feedback:

Please list any suggestions that you have that would help our organization:

1. grow the business,
2. grow the people, and
3. grow the culture.

Individual, Team and Organizational Surveys

The Manager/Leadership Evaluation Form (Figure 7-1, located at the end of
this chapter) allows the individuals who receive the feedback to do a differential diagnosis. Differential diagnosis is made up of feedback that is specific enough that the individual who has been rated knows what he or she needs
to do to improve his or her performance. For example, consider a manager who
is rated low on feedback to employees and does not know what to do to
improve his or her performance. By asking questions both about the frequency and specificity of feedback, we can now do a differential diagnosis.
Manager A may give feedback that is specific enough but is too infrequent.
Manager B may give feedback frequently enough, but is not specific enough.
A differential diagnosis more specifically defines the behaviour that needs to
be changed.

The manager who uses it may want to have the feedback collected by a
neutral third party. You can't say that you are open to feedback and then
punish your staff if they give you some critical feedback—if you do this you
will do significant damage to your credibility.

You don't have to limit this type of feedback to individuals. When David
Rathbun was director of human resources at Maritime Life, he completed
yearly work/attitude surveys. This data allowed Maritime Life to benchmark
itself on its internal and external goals. In areas that were designated for
improvement, task force groups were formed to set and achieve goals. The
questions on the work/attitude survey looked at traditional questions such
as pay, benefits, communications and decision-making in the organization. It
also looked at some less traditional areas of concern. For example, Maritime
Life has a large number of young working mothers on staff. When they were

moving into their new building, the employees suggested that they build a daycare centre and a gym, which they did. One of the most interesting suggestions was to add a small convenience store to the new building's plans. The convenience store would allow people to buy that extra litre of milk, drop off their dry cleaning, or rent a movie without having to make an extra stop on the way home after work. It is for these reasons that Maritime Life was voted as one of the best companies to work for in Canada.

David then took the process one step further. Company employees rated the effectiveness of the Human Resources Department in 45 specific areas. This way, goals were set to increase the effectiveness of individual departments as well as the organization as a whole. David states that this feedback was incredibly important: "It told us where we were doing a great job, a good job and an unsatisfactory job. In some cases the unsatisfactory rating meant that we had to improve our performance and in others it meant that we had a PR problem that had to be taken care of with more accurate and timely communication."

Develop Methods and Opportunities to Maximize Feedback

There is a scene from the movie *The Sixth Sense*, in which Haley Joel Osment plays the role of Cole, an eight-year-old disturbed boy, and Bruce Willis plays the role of Malcolm Crowe, a renowned child psychologist. The scene opens with Cole standing in the entryway of his house and Malcolm sitting in the middle of the living room. Malcolm tries to get his young patient to open up to him by asking Cole if he would like to play a game. The essence of the game is that Malcolm will try to guess what Cole is thinking. If Malcolm guesses correctly, Cole will take a step closer and if Malcolm guesses incorrectly, Cole will take a step back. If Malcolm guesses correctly enough, Cole will sit down and they will have a conversation, if he does not guess correctly enough and Cole reaches the front door of their home, both the game and the session are over.

One of the many things that is so intriguing about this scene is that Malcolm has set it up so that he gets immediate feedback as to the accuracy of his perceptions about Cole. Likewise, Master Negotiators are vigilant for and develop methods and opportunities to maximize the feedback that they receive. This ability is clearly demonstrated in the following two examples.

I once had the opportunity to work with Dalhousie University men's basketball team. Doc Ryan was the head coach. It is safe to say that the coach's job is to be a feedback machine. He or she must constantly give the team members feedback to help improve their ability to play individually and as a team. The amazing thing about Doc Ryan was that he handed out a form after every game. The form asked the players to write down three things Ryan did well as their coach during the game and three suggestions for improvement. This same type of feedback is available to every coach, but how many coaches do you know who actively and systematically solicit feedback from his or her players? Master Coaches and Master Negotiators actively seek out the feedback they need so they can continually improve their abilities.

For Master Negotiators there are no obstacles or excuses that stand between them and their goal of maximizing salient feedback. I met a university vice-president at one of the conferences I was speaking at. Part of my talk concerned salient feedback. The university vice-president told me the following story. The university for which he worked had a very hard-working and dynamic president. The university president was so busy on so many different fronts that he rarely gave the vice-president feedback. So the vice-president asked for a three-hour yearly meeting with the president. During this time, the vice-president went over his accomplishments and real and perceived shortcomings during the past year. The vice-president then asked his president for feedback as to how the president saw his accomplishments, shortcomings and perceived shortcomings for that year. The vice-president told me he always had ample feedback from his staff and his constituents, and that he needed more feedback from the president. In setting up his yearly meetings, he met his needs for more direct feedback from his president and he set it up in such a way that was easy for the president to do. This is not to say that he didn't have necessary conversations with his president during the year, however, the three-hour meeting met his need for a more formal performance review. Exercise 7-2 was developed as a way to increase your salient feedback.

EXERCISE 7-2

Increasing Salient Feedback

List three opportunities that exist for you to receive more feedback at work.

1. _____

_____

_____

2. _____

_____

_____

3. _____

_____

_____

List three opportunities that exist for you to receive more feedback at home.

1. _____

_____

_____

2. _____

_____

_____

3. _____

_____

_____

Seeking Feedback From Spouses, Children and Significant Others

Once or twice a year, when I am feeling particularly secure as a father, I sit my two children down individually and ask them to tell me three things that I am doing well as a father and three targets for improvement. This type of relationship feedback is important for three reasons, firstly what it tells me about me, secondly, what it tells me about my children, and thirdly, what it tells me about my relationships with my children.

I was pleasantly surprised to learn that both my children thought that I helped them to learn responsibility. I was not surprised to learn that both my children thought that I should be more patient. I have now asked them to remind me when they see me being impatient to help me change that aspect of my behaviour.

There is another added benefit. When my children see that I am willing to change an aspect of my behaviour, it increases the likelihood that they will be willing to change an aspect of their behaviour. In cases like this, parents can model behaviour, such as openness and willingness to change, that they would like to see reflected in their children's behaviour.

Variants on the questions are: "What do you like most about yourself?" and "What do you most need to work on?" My son Andrew, who was 12 the first time I asked this question, told me he was "kind." You could have knocked me over with a feather; his self-diagnosis was absolutely spot-on. Even when playing hockey, Andrew is the first one over when a player falls to the ground to help them up. When asked what he most needed to work on, Andrew said that sometimes he is too passive. We then were able to talk about situations where he could be more proactive and how I could help to remind him to do so. Once again, the opportunities to solicit salient feedback exist. Most of us fail to capitalize on those opportunities. Master Negotiatosrs do not!

The third area where asking for salient feedback can change the relationship is learning that it is okay to be open with each other about what one appreciates and about what one does not appreciate about another member of the family. This gives the message that the family system is open rather than closed, which significantly increases the likelihood that those things that need to be talked about in the family will be talked about.

TECHNIQUE 2: LEARNING FROM COACHING, MENTORING AND MASTERMIND GROUPS

There are two ways to find a coach—on purpose and by accident. The first way is to look for someone who has the skills and abilities to be an excellent coach and then ask him or her to coach you.

For example, I wanted to continue to improve my knowledge of the negotiation process and by this time I had taken every course on negotiation that the Harvard Program on Negotiation had to offer. Instead of finding another course on negotiation, I decided that I could learn more from a somewhat different perspective. I therefore decided to study mediation with Suki Starnes and Annette Strug of AMS Mediation Services. From taking this course I realized that "Every time I negotiate, I mediate and every time I mediate, I negotiate." Let me explain. The part that says "Every time I negotiate, I mediate," means that when two people are in conflict and it is clear that the negotiation is not going anywhere, then you need to take a break from the table, bring in an outside mediator, or one of the participants must temporarily move out of the role of negotiator and take on the role of the mediator. Likewise, the part that states, "every time I mediate, I negotiate," means that when I am acting as a mediator, I almost always have to negotiate with at least one party to try a different style of negotiation, one where both parties get at least some of their needs met, and/or where both parties can save face. From this course, I not only learned more about negotiation from a mediator's point of view, which stood me in good stead in all of my future negotiations, I have also asked both Suki and Annette to be my ongoing mediation coaches as I learn more about mediating.

The second way to find a coach is by chance; you just stumble on to someone who could be an ideal coach. For example, I had enrolled in a wonderful weeklong course on Authentic Leadership.[5] As part of the course, we could enrol in various sub-disciplines. The sub-discipline I chose was personal mastery; it was taught by Master Teacher Fred Koffman. During the course, each participant was given the opportunity to have a 20-minute consultation with Fred. The concern that I brought to our conversation was a negotiation with which I was having a great deal of difficulty. As hard as I tried, I just could not come up with options that would be fair to both parties. At the end of our conversation, Fred reminded me that even though it might not be fair, some things are better off not being negotiated. Sometimes you *do* have to walk away from the table. Even with all the right skills, techniques and preparation, Master Negotiators must learn to recognize the signs pointing to "abort mission," and Fred Koffman reminded me of this.

> *Even though it might not be fair, some things are better off not being negotiated.*
>
> **Fred Koffman**

Mastermind groups are groups of like-minded individuals who collectively help each other develop their skills and strategies through peer mentoring. They also hold each other responsible for developing specific goals in specific time frames. To be effective, the group should meet at least once a month. The group that I belong to is made up of six individuals: three professional speakers, two CEOs and a vice-president of successful companies.

One of the purposes of the mastermind group is to assist in and support the accomplishments of those things that would serve as escalators to bring us to the next level of success in our careers. Here is an example: one of the things that I would really like to develop is audiotapes. I have written four books, but also need some audiocassette programs, which would be valuable to me from both a revenue point of view and from a marketing point of view. I have been talking about developing an audiocassette program for a long time. It was well past time for action. Therefore, one of the goals I set with my mastermind group was to complete an audiocassette program by a certain date. Because I set this as an important goal, and made it public in front of people who are important to me, I would lose face if I didn't complete it. Likewise, one of my counterparts in the group is a very talented and eloquent professional speaker. Because he is the CEO of his company and is very active with his church and his family, he has not put pen to paper to develop written descriptions for his presentations. These are absolutely necessary to secure speaking engagements. This is something that two of us in the group do quite well, so when he set his goal to develop three first-rate seminar/keynote descriptions, the other members in the group acted as coaches and mentors. All of the members of our mastermind group, each of whom is a highly motivated individual, stated that membership in the group has made all of us 20 to 30 percent more effective in those areas where we needed to grow. Another member most needs to work on writing a book. Her goal is to write a newsletter and then turn that newsletter into a book. Yet another member wants to specialize in keynotes on leadership and the goal of the rest of the group is to make sure that he does everything in his power to achieve that goal.

Warning! Other people will observe the effect of being in a mastermind group and will want to join. You have to be incredibly selective. This is not a group to mentor people who are at a different stage in development than you are. That can be done in other venues. All of the people in the mastermind group need to be at the same level of development. Of course, you will have different areas of strengths and this is important because you can help each other develop those skills, and/or those skills can be applied to help other members achieve their goals. The easiest way to say this is that mastermind groups work best when made up of peers.

TECHNIQUE 3: LEARN HOW TO THINK LIKE THE EXPERTS

Become a student of the world's best negotiators. We can study the world's best through reading their autobiographies and biographies, and by watching movies and television programs that highlight the accomplishments that these negotiators have achieved through their negotiating and influencing skills. For example, excerpts from the following *Negotiation Newsletter* demonstrate the lessons I learned from reading books and by watching films about Gandhi.[6]

Mahatma Gandhi became one of the world's most famous leaders, advocates and negotiators. The story of how Gandhi came to understand and apply these skills in the context of his philosophy of militant non-violence is fascinating reading for anyone who wants to develop these skills. Two examples, one from very early in his career in South Africa, illustrate the development of Gandhi's remarkable philosophy.

In the first example, the South African government threatened to arrest all Indians who did not carry registration passes. Gandhi and the other Indians in South Africa resisted by refusing to carry these registration passes. "The South Africans arrested so many that it became untenable for South Africa to carry out this policy." As a negotiator, Gandhi knew he could reduce the power of the other side by acquiescing to their pressure tactic rather than resisting it. This was the beginning of militant non-violence. His method was deliberately to break the law, and to organize his followers into a mass movement.

> *As a negotiator, Gandhi knew he could reduce the power of the other side by acquiescing to their pressure tactic rather than resisting it. This was the beginning of militant non-violence.*

The second story relates to one of the most memorable parts of the film *Gandhi,* which takes place when a Hindu man, whose son had been killed in the riots between the Hindus and Muslims, asks Gandhi for help after another riot in which the man killed a Muslim child in revenge. The Hindu man is overwrought with grief at his son's death and abhorrence for his having killed a Muslim child. Gandhi suggests that the Hindu man find an orphaned Muslim boy and raise that boy as a Muslim. This is another example of Gandhi's use of the power of a wise solution to help resolve seemingly irresolvable problems. There are other examples of Gandhi's use of his leadership, negotiating and problem-solving skills such as his advocating to bring an end to India's caste system.

> When he died, Gandhi was what he had always been: a private citizen without wealth, property, title, official position, academic distinction, or scientific achievement. Yet the chiefs of all governments, except the Soviet government, and the heads of all religions paid homage to the thin brown man of seventy-eight in a loincloth.[7]

One of Gandhi's most famous quotes was that "We must become the change we seek in the world." Gandhi's life was a tribute to that quote.

EXERCISE 7-3

Learning from the Experts

List the names of several expert negotiators and influencers you would like to know more about. For example, how they accomplished what they accomplished, the strategies, skills and methods they used to achieve their results, etc. In the second column, beside that person's name, list the resources you will use to research the expert(s) you have chosen. For example, you might want to learn more about historical figures such as Winston Churchill, Mother Teresa or Anwar Sadat. Or your may want to learn about contemporary Master Negotiators such as Paul Tellier, Dawna Ring or Bernd Christmas. You can conduct your research through libraries and on the Internet by reading biographies, autobiographies, etc.

Name of Expert(s)	Resources

TECHNIQUE 4: INTERVIEW THE BEST NEGOTIATORS AND INFLUENCERS

Another proven method to improve our understanding of this process of negotiating and influencing is to interview the best negotiators you know of or can find and who would agree to be interviewed. You can select people who are well-known negotiators and/or influencers, such as business leaders, entrepreneurs, politicians, advocates, etc. Simply ask if you can set up a 15-minute appointment. You can use both your time and their time more effectively if you do some pre-interview homework. Find out as much as you can about a specific negotiation and/or accomplishment by preparing high-yield questions regarding strategies, methods and techniques that they found effective. High-yield questions invite the person you are interviewing to share at the most meaningful level possible what they have learned about the subject at hand, which in this case is about negotiating and influencing skills. Examples of high-yield questions are "What did you learn during negotiating that you would have liked to have known before the negotiation started?" Or "What lessons would you want to make sure were passed on to someone who was entering a similar negotiation in the future?" One of the best ways to develop your understanding of how to ask high-yield questions is to observe the best interviews you know. You can observe people you know personally, as well as people in the media, including Canada's best journalists.

Alternatively, you can list three aspects of negotiating and influencing about which you want to or need to learn more. I used both approaches in interviewing the Master Negotiators who contributed their stories and their expertise in the writing of this book. I also learned and benefited greatly from their experience, and this increased the breadth and depth of my knowledge to a degree for which I could not have hoped.

TECHNIQUE 5: LEARN FROM THE BEST BOOKS, MOVIES, AND COURSES

Learning effective negotiating and influencing skills is a life-long process. In a very real sense, reading this book is only the beginning of that process. To answer the question, "Where do I go from here?" some suggestions on how to find the best information possible follow.

EXERCISE 7-4

Developing Specific Negotiating Skills

Being relatively specific, list three aspects of negotiating and influencing about which you want to or need to learn more. Examples of topics about which you might want to or need to learn more could be learning how to be more diplomatic, flexible or creative. List up to three topics. Under each topic list three to five people's names that you could interview to learn more about each topic. Complete one set of interviews, learn all you can, and then apply some of those lessons before going on to the next topic.

Topic(s):	Resource(s):
1. _____	_____
	_____
	_____
	_____
	_____
2. _____	_____
	_____
	_____
	_____
	_____
3. _____	_____
	_____
	_____
	_____
	_____

From *The Seven Strategies of Master Negotiators* by Brad McRae © 2002, McGraw-Hill Ryerson.

Learning From Books and Films

The Resources of the Masters: An Annotated Bibliography at the end of this book lists over 50 of the best books, articles and movies on negotiating and influencing skills. Each reference is described in enough detail to help you make an informed choice about whether it would be helpful to you in further developing your skills.[8]

Learning From Courses

Excellent courses are available through the Program on Negotiation at the Harvard Law School, the Program on Instruction for Lawyers and McRae Seminars. Each of these institutions and their course offerings are described below.

The Program on Negotiation at the Harvard Law School offers a variety of excellent courses. One of the best is the Program on Negotiation for Senior Executives. Three faculty members from the Project on Negotiation teach this one-and-a-half day course. The course helps the participants to better understand the "Getting to Yes" model through both individual and team negotiation simulations. The simulations provide direct feedback on where your negotiation skills are working well and on where they need to be improved.

Another highly recommended course is William Ury's Dealing with Difficult People and Difficult Situations. Ury is a Master Teacher. The course examines strategies and tactics that can be used against you in a negotiation and effective counter-strategies that you can use when negotiating with difficult people and in difficult situations.

For those interested in teaching negotiation skills, the course Teaching Negotiation in the Corporation will be of interest. This course presents the developmental history and the pedagogy of teaching negotiation skills as taught at the Harvard Project on Negotiation.

For those interested in complex multiple-party, value-laden disputes, I highly recommend Harvard courses such as Dealing with an Angry Public: Protecting Your Reputation and Your Market Share. This course deals with strategies for "resolving conflicts and disputes with dissatisfied customers, potential litigants, and concerned interest groups."[9]

The Program of Instruction for Lawyers offers two intensive five-day courses every summer: the basic course and the advanced course. The student enrolment is approximately 60 percent from the United States; the other 40 percent of students come from other countries. Two-thirds to three-quarters of the students are lawyers; the rest are from various other backgrounds. Being a lawyer is not a prerequisite. The course members spend a great deal of time negotiating. Many of the case studies are scored, so the participants receive immediate feedback as to how well they negotiated compared to others. A highlight of the advanced course is the use of Harvard's advanced technique of videotaped feedback. The length of the course and the sheer number of negotiations that take place ensure that the participants see where they are negotiating well and where improvement is required.[10]

McRae Seminars offers basic and advanced courses on the Seven Strategies of Master Negotiators. Other seminars offered include: Mediation Skills in Business and Organizational Settings and the Consensus Decision-Making Workshop.[11] For more specific information, see About the Author at page 262.

Lastly, most universities and local training organizations offer courses in negotiation, mediation and conflict management. Do not judge a course by its brochure. Use your research and networking skills to find the ones that create the most value!

FIGURE 7-1

Manager/Leadership Evaluation Form

Manager's Name: _____

Please rate your manager or supervisor on the following scales. If you do
not have enough information at the present time to rate your manager
fairly on any of the scales, please circle N/A to the right of the scale.

I find that the goals my manager wants me to work for are:

unclear   **clear**
_____ N/A
1   2   3   4   5   6   7

As a person to work for, I find my manager to be:

disorganized   **organized**
_____ N/A
1   2   3   4   5   6   7

As a person to work with, my manager is:

unmotivated   **very motivated**
_____ N/A
1   2   3   4   5   6   7

In terms of decision-making, my manager:

needs improvement   **is excellent**
_____ N/A
1   2   3   4   5   6   7

I receive feedback from my manager:

infrequently   **frequently**
_____ N/A
1   2   3   4   5   6   7

I receive feedback from my manager that is:

vague   **specific**

_____ N/A

1   2   3   4   5   6   7

My manager's technical understanding of the work I do:

needs improvement   **is excellent**

_____ N/A

1   2   3   4   5   6   7

My manager's understanding of my needs as an employee:

needs improvement   **is excellent**

_____ N/A

1   2   3   4   5   6   7

In dealing with staff, I find my manager to be:

discourteous   **courteous**

_____ N/A

1   2   3   4   5   6   7

My manager delegates the workload:

unfairly   **fairly**

_____ N/A

1   2   3   4   5   6   7

My manager behaves in a way that enhances my feelings of personal
worth and importance:

not at all descriptive   **very descriptive**

_____ N/A

1   2   3   4   5   6   7

My manager behaves in a way that encourages all members of the group
to develop close, mutually satisfying relationships.

not at all descriptive   **very descriptive**

_____ N/A

1   2   3   4   5   6   7

From *The Seven Strategies of Master Negotiators* by Brad McRae © 2002, McGraw-Hill Ryerson.

FIGURE 7-1 . . . *Continued*

My manager behaves in a way that stimulates enthusiasm for meeting the group's goal of excellent performance.

not at all descriptive   **very descriptive**

——————————————————————————————————— N/A

1   2   3   4   5   6   7

My manager behaves in a way that helps achieve goal attainment by such activities as scheduling, coordinating and providing resources, materials and technical knowledge.

not at all descriptive   **very descriptive**

——————————————————————————————————— N/A

1   2   3   4   5   6   7

In terms of his/her ability to listen carefully to what I have to say, I find that my manager:

needs improvement   **is excellent**

——————————————————————————————————— N/A

1   2   3   4   5   6   7

In terms of his/her ability to facilitate a meeting, I find that my manager:

needs improvement   **is excellent**

——————————————————————————————————— N/A

1   2   3   4   5   6   7

In terms of presenting his/her ideas, I find my manager to be:

opinionated   **open-minded**

——————————————————————————————————— N/A

1   2   3   4   5   6   7

My manager is (excellent/unsatisfactory) in his/her ability to be a coach/mentor.

unsatisfactory   **excellent**

——————————————————————————————————— N/A

1   2   3   4   5   6   7

My manager spends (enough/not enough) time coaching me in how to do my job.

not enough   **enough**

						N/A
1	2	3	4	5	6	7

In terms of teamwork and team building, I find that my manager:

needs improvement   **is excellent**

						N/A
1	2	3	4	5	6	7

I find my manager to be (supportive/unsupportive) of the efforts of other departments within this organization.

unsupportive   **supportive**

						N/A
1	2	3	4	5	6	7

My manager spends (enough/not enough) time coaching me on how to advance in my career.

not enough   **enough**

						N/A
1	2	3	4	5	6	7

In terms of performance management, I am evaluated:

unfairly   **fairly**

						N/A
1	2	3	4	5	6	7

Would your manager notice if you put 15 percent more effort into your job?

yes _____   no _____   N/A _____

Would your manager notice if you put 15 percent less effort into your job?

yes _____   no _____   N/A _____

FIGURE 7-1 . . . *Continued*

Please list three specific things you enjoy about working with your manager:

1. _____

_____

2. _____

_____

3. _____

_____

Please list three specific things you have learned from working with your manager:

1. _____

_____

2. _____

_____

3. _____

_____

Please list three specific things that your manager could do to improve his/her managerial performance in your department:

1. _____

_____

2. _____

_____

3. _____

_____

From *The Seven Strategies of Master Negotiators* by Brad McRae © 2002, McGraw-Hill Ryerson.

Please make any suggestions you have for improving this working relationship:

_____

_____

_____

_____

_____

_____

_____

_____

_____

_____

_____

Please list any other suggestions that you have that would help your company:

1. Grow the Business

_____

_____

2. Grow the People

_____

_____

3. Grow the Culture

_____

_____

[1] McCall, Morgan, Michael Lombardo and Ann Morrison. *The Lessons of Experience: How Successful Executives Develop on the Job*. N.Y.: Free Press, 1988.

[2] A smart board is a device that interacts with the computer. The teacher can write class notes on it, project images on it, and then post all of the notes on the Internet for the children to review or see for the first time if they missed a class.

[3] Note Stella's use of objective criteria here.

[4] Director, Contracting, Finance and Administration, Corporate Services, Department of Fisheries and Oceans.

[5] This excellent course is based on Peter Senge's philosophy as articulated in his book, *The Fifth Discipline*. N.Y.: Doubleday, 1990.

[6] Sections of the following were first developed for the *Negotiation Newsletter* (Vol. VII).

[7] Louise Fischer. *Gandhi: His Life and Message for the World*. New York: Mentor, 1954, pp. 7-8.

[8] For a more extensive annotated bibliography, visit **www.bradmcrae.com**.

[9] For more detailed information on these and other course offerings, write to: Program on Negotiation, Harvard Law School, Cambridge, Massachusetts, U.S.A. 02138, phone (617) 239-1111, fax (617) 239-1546, Web site: **http://www.pon.harvard.edu/newpon/main/home/index.php3.**

[10] For more information on this program, contact: Program of Instruction For Lawyers, Harvard Law School, Pound Hall 207, Cambridge, Massachusetts, U.S.A. 02138, phone (617) 495-3187.

[11] Custom-designed courses are also available to meet any organization's specific needs and requirements. For more information, contact: McRae & Associates Inc.; 5880 Spring Garden Road, Suite 400, Halifax, Nova Scotia, B3H 1Y1, phone (902) 423-4680; e-mail: brad@bradmcrae.com; Web site: www.bradmcrae.com. See also the author's biography at p. 262.

CONCLUSION

Be Vigilant for Opportunities

The Power of Determination

All of the negotiation strategies and skills in the world will not help us unless we have the determination to take action and put them into practice. The following story illustrates the power of determination.

I was invited to co-author and co-present a keynote address on the second day of the bi-annual conference on osteogenesis imperfecta, (OI) in San Antonio, Texas. OI is a rare genetic disorder where the bone does not produce enough collagen, which results in brittle bones. It is not uncommon for children with OI to have over 100 fractures growing up, or to spend at least part of their childhood in full body casts. By adulthood, most people with OI are confined to wheelchairs because their limbs have received so many fractures. OI creates a profound dilemma for most of the parents of children with OI. If you do not let your child ride a bike, has he or she fully experienced childhood? If the parents do let their children ride a bike, they could fall off and be in a body cast for six months.

The title of our talk was "OI, from Stigma to Self-Esteem." The keynote speaker on the first day was a man named Paul Hearne. Paul, who himself had OI, shared with the audience his experiences growing up with osteogenesis imperfecta. If I was giving a presentation on developing self-esteem under difficult circumstances, Paul was a living example as the following excerpts from his presentation point out.

Paul said that he missed a lot of schooling due to his frequent fractures. It didn't matter so much in English because he was an avid reader and always managed to catch up. Mathematics, however, was an entirely different matter, because mathematics is sequential. Paul came back to school and found that he had missed key concepts, which made it almost impossible to master the current material. Paul persevered in math and graduated from high school.

Paul was a member of my generation, that is, the hippy generation. One of the rights of passage of those times for many of us was to spend the summer hitchhiking across the country and/or hitchhiking around Europe. So in a wheelchair and with long hair—and against the advice of his parents—Paul decided to hitchhike through Europe.

Paul began his European trip by flying to Berlin. He found the nearest youth hostel to spend the night. Youth hostels are usually quite intriguing. In Stockholm, the youth hostel is an old sailing ship; in Ottawa it is an old jail. In Berlin, it was an old warehouse, which lacked elevators for the hostellers to get from the reception area to the sleeping bunks upstairs. Paul negotiated with the young Berliners who ran the hostel. They would carry him upstairs each night and downstairs each morning, and in return Paul would do their dreaded paperwork.

When Paul returned to the United States after successfully hitchhiking through Europe, he decided to apply to law school. He was granted an interview at the law school that he most wanted to attend. Paul was greeted by the dean of the law school and ushered into an opulent office with burgundy leather chairs and floor to ceiling books.

After the preliminary remarks, the dean told Paul that he was not a strong candidate for law school. The dean gave Paul three reasons. Firstly, most of the court houses had steep steps leading up to the buildings with no elevators; secondly, the jury would feel sorry for Paul and this factor could result in a mistrial, and thirdly, in his wheelchair Paul was only four feet tall. Therefore he could access only the bottom third of the books that were in the law library.

Paul said that he had the feeling that the interview was not going so well. He then asked the dean how many people he was interviewing for law school. The dean said that Paul was the only one, implying the assistant dean was interviewing all of the other candidates. Although Paul's mathematics was one of his weaker areas, he asked the dean how many people were being interviewed for law school. The Dean said 268. Paul said, "That means that you didn't have to interview 267, and with the time that you saved, I guess if I were having trouble getting a book from the upper shelves in the law library, I could call you to help me get it." Paul was accepted into law school.

After law school, Paul became the president and CEO of the Dole Foundation. The purpose of the Dole Foundation is to help physically challenged individuals obtain gainful employment. The unemployment rate for the physically challenged in both Canada and the United States is 60 percent.

Paul's biggest challenge in that position was to help pass a piece of legislation that was entitled the Americans with Disability Act. A friend of Paul's said they would never get it passed. Paul asked his friend if he had ever bought a lottery ticket. His friend said, "Yes." Paul asked his friend the odds of his winning the lottery. His friend said, "Two million to one." Paul asked his friend what he thought Paul's odds of getting the American's with Disabilities Act passed. His friend said "300 to one." Paul said, "Sounds like my odds are better than yours." The Americans with Disabilities Act was passed.

After giving his incredibly inspiring talk, Paul looked out on the audience of over 300 people, some who had OI, others who were the parents of children with OI, and said "I would like to challenge all of us to be vigilant for opportunities."

I have chosen to conclude this book with Paul's words, "**be vigilant for opportunities**." As negotiators, we can build our future: the future of our families, our communities, our states or provinces, our countries, and indeed the future of our planet. Understanding this, Master Negotiators are constantly looking for opportunities. The Master Negotiator maximizes the chance of capitalizing on opportunities by being prepared. Whether by doing background research, by developing optimal solutions, by creating and claiming maximum value, or by knowing their own and the other party's negotiating style, the Master Negotiator keeps an eye on the prize. At the same time, the Master Negotiator works to manage the negotiation process, build strategic alliances within and between the parties and find learning opportunities whenever they present themselves. The process of becoming a Master Negotiator is constant and ongoing.

The way in which Paul lived his life demonstrates that understanding the Seven Strategies is not enough. Paul's determination, like the determination of all of the Master Negotiators I interviewed, is essential to convert the strategies into action. My best advice is to be vigilant for opportunities to learn and enhance your ability to use the Seven Strategies of Master Negotiators. By so doing, you will make yourself a better person and the world a better place.

The Who's Who of
Master Negotiators

LLOYD AXWORTHY, FORMER FOREIGN AFFAIRS MINISTER
Lloyd Axworthy was elected to the House of Commons in 1979 and served as minister of foreign affairs from January, 1996 to October, 2000. He played a strong leadership role in the successful campaigns for a ban on anti-personnel landmines. He is currently serving as director of the Liu Centre for the Study of Global Issues at the University of British Columbia in Vancouver.

BILL BLACK, PRESIDENT AND CHIEF EXECUTIVE OFFICER, MARITIME LIFE
Maritime Life was formed in 1922. By 1961, Maritime Life was considered Canada's fastest growing insurance company when it acquired The Royal Guardians Insurance Company of Montreal. John Hancock Mutual Life Insurance Company of Boston, Massachusetts purchased Maritime Life in 1969. Maritime Life acquired Confederation Life in 1995, Aetna in 1999, and Royal & Sun Alliance Financial in 2001. In 1995, Bill Black became president of Maritime

Life. Maritime Life was ranked by the *Globe and Mail* as one of the 35 best companies to work for in Canada. By 2000, Maritime Life's sales were $1.795 billion.

STELLA CAMPBELL, FORMER CHAIRPERSON, HALIFAX REGIONAL SCHOOL BOARD

The Halifax Regional School Board is the largest school board in Nova Scotia serving more than 58,000 students, in 140 elementary and secondary schools and employing a staff of nearly 5,000. Stella Campbell was first elected to the Halifax Regional School Board in 1994 and assumed the position of chairperson from 1998 to 2000.

BERND CHRISTMAS, CHIEF EXECUTIVE OFFICER, MEMBERTOU BAND

The Membertou Band is a Mi'kmaw First Nations community located in the city of Sydney, Nova Scotia. The Membertou Band offers programs and services to approximately 1,000 members, both on and off reservation lands, including access to initiatives concerning education, social security, health, economic development, human resources, justice and recreation. The band believes that the path of the future incorporates the traditions of the past. The future path is being blazed by community leaders such as Bernd Christmas who assumed the position of CEO in 1996.

ERIC CLAUS, GENERAL MANAGER AND CHIEF EXECUTIVE OFFICER, CO-OP ATLANTIC

CO-OP Atlantic stores serve over 200,000 member families in Atlantic Canada and Quebec. Sales in 2000 were $478 million from wholesale operations, provision of specialized management services, the operation of livestock and poultry feed plants, and the operation of Atlantic Peoples' Housing Ltd. Eric Claus became CEO in 1997 and is credited with helping his company become even more successful in spite of intense competition. For the 2000 business year, sales increased by 8 percent.

JANET CONNERS, AIDS ACTIVIST

Between 1993 and 1999, Janet Conners was front and centre in the media as the principal spokesperson for people who had been secondarily infected with HIV. During that time she proved herself to be a woman of extraordinary courage, warmth and compassion. She led a successful fight to compensate innocent people who were secondarily infected with HIV through tainted blood and became a true Canadian hero in the process. On October 12, 2001, Janet and Randy (posthumously) Conners received the Meritorious Service Medal (civil division) from the Governor General of Canada.

NEVILLE GILFOY, PUBLISHER, ATLANTIC PROGRESS MAGAZINE

The magazine business is a notoriously difficult business to make work. Through his creative solutions and effective negotiation skills, Neville Gilfoy is a distinct exception. Started in 1994, Progress Corp. publishes four magazines and three annuals each year. *Atlantic Progress* magazine has a current circulation of 25,000, and Progress Corp's conference for leading entrepreneurs attracts over 200 business leaders every year.

RUTH GOLDBLOOM, ORDER OF CANADA RECIPIENT FOR PIER 21

Ruth Goldbloom was the driving force in the development of Pier 21. She led the fundraising efforts that raised over $9 million so Pier 21 could be reopened. The Pier 21 National Historic Site is a tribute to the immigrants who have passed through its doors and helped develop Canada into a diverse and strong nation. Between 1928 and 1971, over one million immigrants and 58,000 War Brides entered Canada and close to 500,000 military personnel, who served overseas during World War II, passed through Pier 21. Pier 21 National Historic Site was named the Best New Attraction in Canada in 2001.

KEVIN HAMM, CHIEF EXECUTIVE OFFICER, PHARMASAVE ATLANTIC

Pharmasave Atlantic is a subsidiary of Pharmasave Drugs (National) Ltd., a national franchise of 300 independently owned drugstores. With over

70 drugstores in Atlantic Canada, Pharmasave Atlantic had sales of over $187 million in 2000, an increase of 3 percent over 1999. Kevin Hamm became CEO of Pharmasave Atlantic in 1994.

BUZZ HARGROVE, PRESIDENT OF THE CANADIAN AUTO WORKERS' UNION

The CAW is the largest private sector union in Canada, representing 250,000 workers in auto assembly, auto parts manufacturing, aerospace, shipbuilding, fisheries, railway transportation, airlines, mining, electrical products, retail, health care and hospitality. The members are organized into 282 local unions and over 1,600 bargaining units. Buzz Hargrove became president of the CAW in 1992.

FRANK KING, THE XVTH WINTER OLYMPICS

Frank King was the driving force behind Calgary's winning bid to host the first Winter Olympics in Canada. He negotiated for and oversaw the construction of $350 million worth of facilities and put on the best Winter Olympics ever. In place of the usual deficit after the Games, the Calgary Winter Olympics left an operating profit of $46 million; this money was used to finance sports activities in Calgary and across the country. In recognition of this achievement, Frank King was inducted into the Order of Canada in 1988.

MAJOR-GENERAL (RETIRED) LEWIS MACKENZIE, UN PEACEKEEPER, BOSNIA

Major-General Lewis MacKenzie spent 33 years in the Canadian military, serving at posts in Germany with NATO forces and having nine tours of peacekeeping in such areas as the Gaza Strip, Cyprus, Vietnam, Egypt and Central America. In 1992, MacKenzie was appointed the chief of staff of the United Nations Protection Force in Yugoslavia. In May, 1992 he created and assumed command of Sector Sarajevo and, in spite of war, with a contingent of troops from 31 nations, managed to open the Sarajevo airport for the delivery of humanitarian aid. As a result, Major-General MacKenzie became the only member of the Canadian Armed Forces to be awarded a second Meritorious Service Cross.

FRANK MCKENNA, FORMER PREMIER OF NEW BRUNSWICK

Frank McKenna was the premier of New Brunswick from 1987 to 1997. During that time, he worked tirelessly on changing the image New Brunswickers had of themselves and of their province. His vision was backed by negotiation after negotiation, no matter how big or how small—with businesses in Canada and around the world—to bring jobs to New Brunswick. One result of his efforts was that New Brunswick became the call centre capital of Canada. By the summer of 1999, over 8,000 jobs had been created in New Brunswick in over 55 call centres.

DAVID MOWAT, CHIEF EXECUTIVE OFFICER, VANCOUVER CITY SAVINGS CREDIT UNION

Vancouver City Savings Credit Union was founded in 1946 to provide financial services to people in Vancouver and has grown to be Canada's largest credit union with $7 billion in assets and 269,000 members. Net earnings for 2000 were $21 million. VanCity is well-known for its social responsibility. It publishes a social audit on VanCity's impact on members, employees, the community and the environment. VanCity also has an EnviroFund that uses a minimum of 5 percent of VanCity's VISA card profits to sustain the environment.

DAVID RATHBUN, CHIEF HUMAN RESOURCES OFFICER OF ALIANT INC.

Aliant Inc. is the result of the merger of MTT of Nova Scotia, IslandTel of Prince Edward Island, NBTel of New Brunswick and NewTel of Newfoundland and Labrador. Aliant provides integrated communications and information technology solutions through subsidiary companies operating worldwide. Aliant has over 10,000 employees and had sales of $2.3 billion in 2000, up 12 percent from the previous year.

DAWNA RING, FEMINIST LAWYER AND LEGAL COUNCIL TO THE KREVER COMMISSION

Dawna Ring has been practising law for 20 years. She represented AIDS activist Janet Conners and all of the people who were secondarily infected with tainted blood before the Krever inquiry into Canada's blood system, participating in the various challenges to the Supreme Court. A colleague described Dawna as follows: "[it is] her tenacious and principled advocacy [that] has earned her a place among Canada's finest female lawyers. I would adopt John Whittier's words and say that she is 'the hope of all who suffer, the dread of all who wrong.'" She was also part of the legal team for the Hepatitis C 86-90 Class Action suit and was a member of the National Negotiating Team and co-chaired the Disease Modeling and Damages Committee.

ISADORE SHARP, CHAIRMAN AND CHIEF EXECUTIVE OFFICER, FOUR SEASONS HOTELS INC.

Isadore Sharp was trained as an architect and worked in his father's construction company before founding Four Seasons Hotels in 1960, with the opening of his first property on Jarvis Street in downtown Toronto. The Four Seasons Hotels and Resorts now manage 50 luxury hotels in 22 countries, with 17 additional properties currently under construction. Isadore Sharp is very active on numerous boards and is currently director of the National Terry Fox Run, the Terry Fox Humanitarian Award Program and numerous additional boards. His vision was to provide the global business traveller with round-the-clock personalized service. This vision has resulted in Four Seasons being recognized as one of the "Top 100 Companies to Work for in America" by *Fortune* magazine.

DR. NICHOLAS STEINMETZ, ASSOCIATE EXECUTIVE DIRECTOR FOR PLANNING, McGILL UNIVERSITY HEALTH CENTRE

Nicolas Steinmetz was the executive director of the Montreal Children's Hospital. He convinced five Montreal hospitals: the Montreal Children's, Montreal General, Montreal Neurological, Montreal Chest and the Royal Victoria Hospitals, as well as the government of Quebec, to build a new state-of-the-art teaching hospital that would combine these five hospitals on one site. When the new McGill University Health Centre opens in 2006, it will be a world-class institution in large part as a result of Dr. Steinmetz's leadership, vision and negotiating skills.

HAROLD TAYLOR, PRESIDENT AND CHIEF EXECUTIVE OFFICER, HAROLD TAYLOR TIME CONSULTANTS INC.

Harold Taylor is a certified speaking professional and one of a select few inducted into the Canadian Association of Professional Speakers' Hall of Fame. He is also one of North America's leading experts in time management, having written 13 books and hundreds of articles.

PAUL TELLIER, PRESIDENT AND CHIEF EXECUTIVE OFFICER, CANADIAN NATIONAL RAILROAD

Paul Tellier was appointed president and CEO and a director of the Canadian National Railway in 1992. Prior to his appointment, he had been clerk of the Privy Council and secretary to the Cabinet of the government of Canada. Paul Tellier was appointed Companion of the Order of Canada in 1993 and is currently director of numerous Canadian companies. In 1997, he was chosen by *Railway Age* as "Railroader of the Year," in 1998 his Canadian peers elected him as the "CEO of the Year" and in 2000 he was named "Personality of the Year" by the newspaper *Les Affaires*. CN employs nearly 25,000 people in Canada and the United States, with over 29,000 route kilometres of track and has earned $5.4 billion in revenue in 2000.

ANNETTE VERSCHUREN, PRESIDENT, HOME DEPOT CANADA

Home Depot Canada is a subsidiary of Home Depot Inc. in the United States and operates 60 stores in Canada with estimated sales of $2.3 billion. Annette Verschuren joined Home Depot Canada in 1996 and has built it into one of this country's most successful "big box" retailers. Annette is currently a board member of Sobey's Inc., the Retail Council of Canada, Mount Allison University and Habitat for Humanity.

Resources from the Masters: An Annotated Bibliography

You can save a great deal of time by reading the right book or using other references at the right time. The following annotated bibliography is designed to help the reader select the best references to aid in the development of his or her negotiating and influencing skills.

BOOKS AND ARTICLES[1]

Augustine, N. R. 1997. Reshaping an Industry: Lockheed Martin's survival story. *Harvard Business Review* (May-June).

   In this insightful article, Augustine chronicles how the U.S. defence industry decreased procurement by more than 60 percent since 1989 as a result of the end of the Cold War. Consequently, 15 major companies were downsized and merged into four. In this article, the author describes 12 essential steps that led Lockheed through this difficult time and on to phenomenal success.

Axelrod, R. 1984. *The Evolution of Cooperation*. New York: Basic Books, Inc.

   The Evolution of Cooperation is an academic book about the conditions under which cooperation evolves. It offers valuable insights illustrated by wonderful examples. One of the best examples is Axelrod's description of the way in which the English and German armies cooperated to minimize the number of fatalities for both sides during the trench warfare of World War I—that is, until the generals on both sides put a stop to it. The reader may find this book to be somewhat academic in parts and therefore may wish to read only those parts that he or she finds particularly worthwhile.

Badaracco, J. 1997. *Defining Moments: When managers must choose between right and right.* Boston, Mass.: Harvard Business School Press.

Perhaps the most neglected aspect of manager and leadership development is ethics. The intriguing examples of negotiating in excruciatingly difficult situations presented in this book are as engrossing as the most well-written mystery novel.

Bazerman, M.H. and M.A. Neale. 1992. *Negotiating Rationally.* Toronto: Maxwell MacMillan Canada.

Negotiating Rationally is both intellectually stimulating and fun to read. The authors illustrate each learning point with such quick-witted examples of where very bright, well-intentioned individuals negotiated less effectively than they could and should have. The book is divided into three parts. Part I examines seven common negotiating mistakes. Part II examines a rational framework for negotiation, and Part III presents the reader with a framework for simplifying complex negotiations.

Bolles, R.N. 2000. *What Color is Your Parachute?* Berkeley, Calif.: Ten Speed Press.

You can find expert advice on negotiating your salary and on negotiating a raise in Richard Bolles' *What Color is Your Parachute?* The author offers sound advice (updated annually) that is both fun and easy to read.

Breslin, W. and J. Rubin, eds. 1995. *Negotiation Theory and Practice.* Cambridge, Mass.: Program on Negotiation at Harvard Law School.

Negotiation Theory and Practice is a selection of articles that covers the nature of conflict and negotiation; organizing your team; getting to the table prepared; the negotiation context; culture, race, gender, and style; multilateral negotiation; and third-party intervention. The book also serves as a reference whenever we run into difficulties negotiating or mediating and as an introduction to many of the authors and practitioners in the field, some of whom the reader may decide to study in greater detail.

Carter, J. 1989. *Nasty People: How to stop being hurt by them without becoming one of them*. Chicago: Contemporary Books, Inc.

Nasty People is an excellent book on dealing with difficult people with particular emphasis on how to disarm them.

Cialdini, R.B. 1993. *Influence: The psychology of persuasion*. New York: William Morrow and Co.

Influence: The psychology of persuasion is one of those infrequent non-fiction books that is as hard to put down as a favourite novel. This book is a joy to read: Cialdini is an outstanding storyteller, an excellent writer and an avid collector of some of the world's best psychological research. Each of the six influence strategies in this book is illustrated with interesting and instructive stories. This book should be required reading for all serious students of persuasion, negotiation and communication.

Chilton, D. 1998. *The Wealthy Barber: Everyone's commonsense guide to becoming financially independent*. 3d ed. Rocklin, CA: Prima Publishing.

Some of the most difficult negotiations couples have concern money: how to spend it, how to save it, and how to plan or not to plan for the future. Many books on financial planning are difficult to read. *The Wealthy Barber* is not only fun to read, it also offers sound financial advice. Most importantly, the book can play the role of a neutral third party whose opinions can help couples get away from positional bargaining. (*See also* McCurdy's *How Much is Enough?*)

Coloroso, B. 2001. *Kids are Worth It! Giving your kid the gift of inner discipline*. Revised edition, Toronto: Penguin Books of Canada.

In *Kids are Worth It!*, Barbara Coloroso has mastered the art of developing multi-options that can help parents negotiate with their children on more equal terms. In this wonderful book she gives expert advice on negotiating with children in such potentially contentious areas as: chores, discipline, mealtime, bedtime, fighting, allowance, teenage rebellion and sex education. The contents of the book are also available on audiocassette and video from Kids Are Worth It!, P.O. Box 621108, Littleton, CO, USA, 80162, or by phoning (800) 729-1588, or visiting **www.kidsareworthit.com**.

Eisenhardt, K., J. Kahwajy and L.J. Bourgeois. 1997. How Top Management Teams can have a Good Fight. *Harvard Business Review* (July-Aug.).

The authors studied conflict and decision-making in 12 high technology companies, all of which "competed in fast changing, competitive global markets . . . [and] had to make high-stakes decisions in the face of considerable uncertainty and under pressure to move quickly." The six-part model that is presented in this article will help all decision-makers develop a decision-making process that they can use confidently to better manage conflict and negotiate effectively within organizations.

Fink, S. 1986. *Crisis Management: Planning for the inevitable.* New York: American Management Assn.

Crisis Management is a book that examines the four stages of crises and suggests more effective ways of dealing with them. The critical importance of effective leadership, communication and negotiating skills during each stage make it fascinating to read. Detailed examples, such as the Three Mile Island crisis, the Johnson & Johnson's Tylenol poisoning, and Union Carbide's catastrophe in Bhopal, illustrate both how to use these skills and the perils that await any CEO and management team who do not use them.

Fisher, R. and W. Ury. 1981. *Getting to Yes: Negotiating agreement without giving in.* Edited by B. Patton. Boston: Houghton Mifflin [—. 1997. 2d ed. London: Arrow Business Books, c. 1991].

Getting to Yes is the most widely read book on the subject of negotiation. It explains the philosophy behind principle-based/interest-based negotiating. *Getting to Yes* is a must-read for anyone interested in improving his or her understanding of the negotiating process. The second edition also contains a section on the 10 most frequently asked questions about the "Getting To Yes" approach.

Gladwell, M. 2000. *The Tipping Point: How little things can make a big difference.* Boston: Little Brown and Co.

A tipping point is a critical point where an epidemic will either grow to full-blown proportions or peters out. This book examines how social epidemics function in the same way. *The Tipping Point* is masterfully researched and written. Leaders, influencers and negotiators will all learn valuable lessons on how to develop the critical mass support necessary to bring their goals and objectives to fruition.

Goleman, D. 1995. *Emotional Intelligence*. New York: Bantam Books.

Emotional Intelligence is a national best seller and for good reason. The major premise of the book is that while one's IQ (intelligence quotient) may facilitate finding a job, one's EQ (emotional intelligence) has the greatest impact on promotability. Emotional intelligence is defined as how well an individual gets along with others and how well one manages himself or herself, all of which are critical to successful negotiations. To learn more about emotional intelligence at work, in marriages and in raising children, this book is an excellent place to start. See also Goleman's *Working with Emotional Intelligence*, which was published by the same publisher in 1998.

Hall, L., ed. 1993. *Negotiation: Strategies for mutual gain: the basic seminar of the Harvard program on negotiation*. Newbury Park, CA: Sage Publications, Inc.

Negotiation: Strategies for mutual gain is a collection of articles by people who have taught at the Harvard Program on Negotiation. The book covers a wide variety of topics from labour management negotiations to resolving environmental disputes. The book is well written and is a good introduction to the 12 authors who have contributed their work.

Holbrooke, R. 1998. *To End a War*. New York: Random House.

Richard Holbrooke and his team were given the mandate to negotiate a peace accord that would end the war in Bosnia-Herzegovina. Holbrooke's book, *To End a War*, portrays their efforts in "one of the toughest negotiations of modern times." Students of negotiation will be fascinated by the flexibility Holbrooke demonstrates in his negotiation style. He can be extremely diplomatic one minute and as tough as nails the next. What fascinated me most was that by the end of the book, I still wasn't sure what Holbrooke's primary negotiating style was. Holbrooke's ability to be diplomatic, to use force and to be unpredictable made him a worthy opponent to Serbia's Milosevic, which makes this book one of the most fascinating reads on the war in Bosnia.

Kotter, J. 1996. *Leading Change*. Boston, Mass.: Harvard Business School Press.

It is during times of change and in the aftermath of change that one really needs to have his or her negotiating skills well honed, but this is not enough. Effective leaders, managers and negotiators also have to have a very good understanding of the process of change. To this end, John Kotter's book, *Leading Change*, is essential reading.

Krannich, R.L. 1994. *Change your Job: Change your Life: High impact strategies for finding great jobs in the 90's.* Manassas Park, VA: Impact Publications [—. 1999. *Change your job: Change your life: High impact strategies for finding great jobs in the decade ahead.* 7th ed. Manassas Park, VA.

Krannich's book *Change your Job: Change your Life* is a very positive, thorough, well-written and well-researched book on how to decide what you want from your career and how to get it. According to the author, one of the most important negotiations one will face surrounds the negotiation for one's salary. Salary negotiations not only determine one's present income, but can also have a large impact on one's future incomes. Salary negotiations are covered in Chapter 15 of this book.

Lax, D.A. and J.K. Sebenius. 1986. *The Manager as Negotiator: Bargaining for cooperation and competitive gain.* New York: Free Press.

The Manager as Negotiator is devoted primarily to negotiating in business and organizational settings. The core negotiating concepts of creating and claiming value, which underlie all negotiations, are presented in this text. Creating value is defined as developing creative solutions and expanding the pie to best meet all of the parties' needs. Claiming value is defined as how well each negotiator gets his or her needs, wants and aspirations met through the negotiating process. The book is well written and contains a wealth of information. The reader should note that this is a very academic read and it may take some time to get through it. However, it is worth the effort.

Lott, L. and R. Intner. 1997. *Chores Without Wars: Turning dad and kids from reluctant stick-in-the-muds to enthusiastic team players.* Rocklin, CA: Prima Publishing.

This book covers the area of getting kids to do chores in all types of families from traditional to single parent to blended. An abundance of options are described to help parents make what is in many families a difficult task into a fun and cooperative environment. One of the sections that most hit home for me was on getting adolescents involved in family life.

McCurdy, D. 2001. *How Much is Enough? Balancing today's needs with tomorrow's retirement goals.* Toronto, ON: McGraw-Hill Ryerson.

Here is a book on retirement planning that is actually fun to read. The book begins with a delightful test of the reader's attitude toward money, which is then scored into four types: Spenders, Builders, Givers and Savers. There are great examples of each of the four types and sound advice on how to benefit from your type as well as pitfalls to avoid. The book goes on to show how marital and relationship difficulties can result from our unconscious attitudes towards money and how to more effectively negotiate our differences.

McRae, B.C. 1998. *Negotiating and Influencing Skills: The art of creating and claiming value*. Thousand Oaks, CA: Sage Publications, Inc.

The purpose of *Negotiating and Influencing Skills* is to help the reader develop and enhance his or her negotiating and influencing skills. There are three reasons why effective negotiating and influencing skills are difficult to learn. Firstly, we can think of the negotiating and influencing skills set as a complex network of skills. Like a symphony orchestra, each skill must work harmoniously and congruently with all the others in order to produce the desired result. Secondly, there is the matter of timing, the very skill that would be used in step one of the negotiating process to help move that negotiation to resolution could meet with disastrous results if one were to use it at step 10. Lastly, the art of effective negotiating is filled with paradoxes. A good negotiator must have the cognitive skills to create value and to claim value, the interpersonal skills to be assertive and empathic, and the wisdom to know when to exercise control and when to let the negotiating process control the outcome. This book contains practical theory, illustrative examples and specifically designed exercises to help the reader fully understand his or her negotiating style, understand where it is working and develop corrective actions to improve areas of concern.

Ozawa, C.P. and L. Susskind. 1985. Mediating Science-Intensive Public Policy Disputes. *Journal of Policy Analysis and Management* (5(1)): 23-39.

In this seminal article Ozawa and Susskind differentiate between advocacy science (where science is used to intensify a conflict and move the parties deeper into positional bargaining) and neutral fact-finding (where science is used to help resolve conflicts). The authors first look at four reasons why scientists disagree: miscommunication, differences in the design of scientific inquiries, error in the inquiry and differences in the interpretation of findings. The authors then make three recommendations that can help resolve science-intensive policy disputes using information sharing, joint fact-finding and collaborative model building.

Perkins, D.N.T., *et al.* 2000. *Leading at the Edge: Leadership lessons from the extraordinary saga of Shackleton's Antarctic expedition.* New York: American Management Assn.

Leading at the Edge examines how a select number of individuals learned how to lead, negotiate and persuade in extreme conditions where their very survival and that of fellow members of the expedition were at stake and the lessons that can be extrapolated from this type of experience to help each of us and the organizations we work for perform at peak performance. If you would like to learn about leadership, peak individual and team performance and the negotiating and influencing skills that are necessary to bring them to fruition in a well-written book with ample servings of drama and adventure, then this book is for you.

Phillips, D. 1992. *Lincoln on Leadership: Executive strategies for tough times.* New York: Warner Books.

Lincoln on Leadership is a remarkable book about the leadership, mediation and negotiating style of one of America's greatest presidents. Particularly interesting is Lincoln's ability to confront others without the need for those people to lose face. *Lincoln on Leadership* is a very informative and readable book about the use of principled leadership and negotiation in extremely difficult times.

Phillips, D.T. 1999. *Martin Luther King, Jr. on Leadership: Inspiration & wisdom for challenging times.* New York: Warner Books.

Martin Luther King, Jr. on Leadership, like *Lincoln on Leadership*, is a remarkably well-written and researched book. Once again, the author draws important lessons for today's leaders, negotiators and advocates. Chapter 12, "Negotiation and Compromise," is particularly interesting for negotiators and advocates.

Pollan, S.M. and M. Levine. 2000. *Turning No into Yes: Six steps to solving your financial problems (so you can stop worrying).* New York: HarperBusiness.

Don't let the subtitle of this book fool you. This book is one of the best books I have found about developing a sound philosophy and methodology of problem solving. It is so sound that I have used it successfully with myself and with my clients. The six steps for turning no into yes are:

1) one problem at a time; 2) focus on facts, not feelings; 3) become an expert; 4) create an environment of trust; 5) turn no into yes; and 6) take charge of your life. For all negotiators, leaders and problem solvers, this book is a must read. It will help us better solve our own problems as well as the problems of those with whom we come into contact.

Pruitt, D.G. and J.Z. Rubin. 1986. *Social Conflict: Escalation, stalemate, and settlement.* New York: Random House [J.Z. Rubin, D.G. Pruit and S.H. Kim. 1994. *Social Conflict: Escalation, stalemate, and settlement.* 2d ed. New York: McGraw-Hill].

Social Conflict is a classic book on conflict resolution. It looks at conflict as if it were a three-act play where Act I is escalation, Act II is stalemate and Act III is resolution to the conflict. This book contains a lot of information on the theory of conflict and conflict resolution, and, wherever possible, the theory is supported by applied research. This book is also very well written, although it may be too academic for some readers.

Rubin, J.Z. 1982. Caught by Choice: The psychological snares we set ourselves. *The Sciences* (22(7)): 18-21.

If writing is a craft, then Rubin's article is one of the most well-crafted articles I have ever had the pleasure of reading. The major premise of the article is that we all become victims by falling into various psychological traps. The traps can be anything, like the proverbial lobster trap, that is easier to get into than out of. Three examples of psychological entrapment are: 1) staying on the phone too long when trying to confirm an airline reservation ticket or get technical assistance. By the time we have invested 10 to 15 minutes waiting, it seems plain wrong to hang up; 2) we continue to pour money into an old car to help justify the money already spent; and 3) we can become trapped into staying in a relationship or a job that has long ceased to bring us any satisfaction, just because we have already invested so much in it. In this seminal article, Rubin presents techniques and strategies that we can use to avoid entrapment. For all serious students of negotiation, leadership and developing the most satisfying life possible, this article is a must read.

Russo, E. and P. Schoemaker. 1989. *Decision Traps: Ten barriers to brilliant decision-making and how to overcome them.* New York: Doubleday/Currency.

Negotiators have to make countless decisions and the better the quality of the decision-making, the better the negotiation outcome. This book analyzes 10 principles that aid in effective decision-making and each principle is illustrated by memorable examples. By helping the reader become a better decision-maker, this book will help him or her become a better negotiator.

Shell, G.R. 1999. *Bargaining for Advantage: Negotiation strategies for reasonable people*. New York: Viking.

The author describes his philosophy of negotiation best in his own words where he says that, "Negotiation is, in short, a kind of universal dance with four stages or steps. And it works best when both parties are experienced dancers." With sound theory and some of the best examples to be found in any book on negotiating and influencing, this book is a must read.

Stone, D., B. Patton and S. Heen. 1999. *Difficult Conversations: How to discuss what matters most*. New York: Viking.

Difficult Conversations is one of those rare books that adds new and very practical insights into one of our most fundamental activities—human communication. This book is full of exquisite examples of difficult conversations that can take place both at work and at home. The following example illustrates the types of difficult conversation the reader will encounter in this book: "You overheard your mother-in-law telling a neighbour that your sons are spoiled and undisciplined. As you prepare to spend the holidays at her house, you're not sure the two of you can get through the week without a confrontation." This book teaches how to manage difficult conversations in a more helpful, constructive and appropriate manner.

Susskind, L. and J. Cruikshank. 1987. *Breaking the Impasse: Consensual approaches to resolving public disputes*. New York: Basic Books.

Breaking the Impasse is a classic in the field of dispute resolution. Susskind and Cruikshank describe a three-part model, which is designed to help multiple parties resolve value-laden disputes where the participants often have entrenched positions. Well-described case studies illustrate each stage of the model. This book is a must-read for anyone interested in negotiating and/or mediating disputes.

Susskind, L. and P. Field. 1996. *Dealing with an Angry Public: The mutual gains approach to resolving disputes*. New York: Free Press.

Dealing with an Angry Public continues the groundbreaking work that *Breaking the Impasse* began, as it further develops and documents the use of the mutual gains approach for resolving multiple-party, value-based disputes. This book contains detailed examples illustrating how this approach has helped to resolve entrenched disputes. Intriguing case studies help the reader understand the principles of consensus decision-making between groups whose interests appear to be extremely adversarial. The book presents clear guidelines of what to do and what not to do to de-escalate differences and foster the consensus decision-making process.

Ury, W. 1991. *Getting Past No: Negotiating with difficult people*. New York: Bantam Books.

I have seen William Ury negotiate and he is indeed a master negotiator. How does he do it? Ury looks at problems as if they were multi-faceted diamonds. He is able to look at problems from every viewpoint without becoming emotionally attached to any of them. He is also able to move from one viewpoint to another with the same fluidity with which Wayne Gretzky skates. Ury's abilities as a negotiator and a problem-solver and the five-part method he has developed are fully explained in this wonderful book. Ury himself describes this book as follows, "If *Getting to Yes* is how to do the negotiation dance, then *Getting Past No* explains how to get that reluctant dance partner onto the dance floor." This book is a must-read for anyone who wants to better understand the negotiating process and learn about strategies and techniques to improve his or her skills.

Ury, W.L., J.M. Brett and S.B. Goldberg. 1993. *Getting Disputes Resolved: Designing systems to cut the costs of conflict*. Cambridge, Mass.: Program on Negotiation at Harvard Law School.

As the title indicates, this book is about designing systems to help resolve disputes. One of the principles of total quality management is that 85 percent of work-site problems are procedural and only 15 percent are due to the people involved. Therefore, if we can develop better procedures, we can systematically lessen the number of disputes and put into place better mechanisms for resolving them. This book has excellent examples that illustrate the principles involved.

Walton, R., J. Cutcher-Gershenfeld and R.B. McKersie. 1994. *Strategic Negotiations: A theory of change in labor-management relations*. Boston, Mass.: Harvard Business School Press.

An important area where interest-based negotiations have had far less influence is in labour-management negotiations. In Part I, the authors examine the conditions under which cooperative or adversarial negotiations take place and the effects of global competition on labour-management negotiations. Part II examines 13 cases of negotiated change in three industries: pulp and paper, automobile supply and railroads. Part III develops a model of strategic choices, while Part IV looks at tactical choices and negotiating dynamics. This book's approach is highly academic, however, the reader is rewarded with many well-developed insights into the societal forces that are fostering and forcing changes in the way management and labour negotiate fundamental changes in their substantive and social contracts.

Zartman, W.I. and M.R. Berman. 1982. *The Practical Negotiator*. New Haven, Conn.: Yale University Press.

Zartman and Berman's book is a classic in the field of international negotiations. The authors define international negotiations as "a process in which divergent values are combined into an agreed decision, and it is based on the idea that there are appropriate stages, sequences, behaviours, and tactics that can be identified and used to improve the conduct of negotiations and better the chances of success" (pp. 1-2). Zartman and Berman masterfully define the three stages of negotiation as: 1) bringing about negotiation: the Diagnostic Phase; 2) defining solutions: the Formula Phase; and 3) working out agreements: the Detail Phase. They also identify the skills that one needs to master to become a Master Negotiator at each stage.

MOVIES

Apollo 13 (1995).

Apollo 13 tells the dramatic story of the ill-fated Apollo 13 mission and its terrifying return to Earth. Among the many crises the crew faced was a problem concerning too much carbon dioxide build-up. A team on the ground had to solve this problem with the limited parts that were already on board the module. Shared leadership, teamwork and the fashioning of creative options from limited resources saved the day. There is a strong parallel from the film to the world of negotiating in that these same three factors are necessary to make many negotiations and mediations successful.

The Chosen (1981).

The Chosen is the story about the development of a deep friendship between two young Jewish men and the ensuing conflict their friendship means for their respective families. This superb film also explores the universal tensions that are created in father/son relationships, and the parenting, coaching, mentoring and negotiating skills that are required to overcome them.

Dances with Wolves (1990).

Dances with Wolves contains excellent examples that demonstrate consensus decision-making, respectful listening, making sure that all parties have a chance to speak and giving credit to the person who spoke before, in Native North American culture. There are also examples of how a failure to understand the other party's culture, and the other party's behaviours based on that culture, can lead to disastrous results.

Disclosure (1994).

The central themes of the movie *Disclosure* are the competition for power and prestige and the use of charges of sexual harassment to help secure one's power and position. A great deal of the plot of the film centres on a mediation in which the two main characters accuse each other of sexual harassment. It looks like a good case of his word against hers, until one of the characters uses the power of preparation and objective criteria to prove their case. The film also demonstrates that there is no such thing as a minor discretion. This film combines learning and entertainment in a package that is well worth viewing.

A Few Good Men (1992).

A Few Good Men is a story about moral leadership and advocacy and their role in a U.S. military court marshal. The film demonstrates the importance of research, preparation, teamwork and intuition, which help bring about a successful resolution to the conflict that is at the centre of this film. The film also demonstrates the hard choices that have to be made between following orders and following one's conscience. A young lawyer must make a choice between following orders and doing what he believes is right, even though doing so may have dire consequences to his career.

Gandhi (1982).

This is a classic movie about leadership, advocacy, the power of the press, the power of principled negotiating and the power of the word to heal. One of the most memorable parts of the film takes place when a Hindu man asks Gandhi for help. The incident occurs after the Muslim/Hindu riots in which the Hindu man, whose own son had been killed by Muslims, kills a Muslim child in revenge. The Hindu man is overwrought with grief for his son's death and revulsion for his own murderous vengeance. In seeking a wise solution, Gandhi suggests that the Hindu man find an orphaned Muslim boy and raise that boy as a Muslim. This is but one example of Gandhi's seeking wise solutions to seemingly irreconcilable conflicts.

The Insider (1999).

The Insider is a film about the costs and rewards of telling the truth. Specifically, it is about one man's decision to tell the truth about his insider knowledge about the tobacco industry, the addictiveness of tobacco and who knew what when. By the time the film ends, it has chronicled the cost of telling and/or of not telling the truth for the insider—a former research scientist at a tobacco company—for his family, for the president and CEO of the tobacco company and for the media. This film, which was one of the best films of 1999, documented the critical importance of wise decision-making, credibility, political influence versus consumer advocacy, and the power of truth versus the power of deception when negotiating.

Judgment at Nuremberg (1961).

This film centres on the trial of four senior judges in the Third Reich for crimes against humanity. One of the major themes of the movie is the moral dilemma of the Nuremberg judges who are trying the four Third Reich judges. The dilemma stems from determining which moral and ethical standards apply to this case. The lawyer who is defending the Third Reich states that the accused's job was to apply the law, not make the law; and that it is the German people who are on trial more so than the Nazi judges. This film is truly about the ethics of behaviour and how best to determine standards in difficult and ambiguous situations. This film is well worth seeing for anyone interested in improving his or her skills in negotiating, advocating and moral leadership.

The Hurricane (1999).

The Hurricane is the story about a black champion prizefighter who was wrongfully given life imprisonment for murders he did not commit and a group of Canadians who used their skills in advocacy, negotiation and leadership to make sure that justice was served. One of the interesting side notes to the film is that through attention to detail and their strong sense of commitment, the understated Canadians succeeded where high profile American celebrities did not.

The Miracle Worker (1962).

The Miracle Worker documents the critical importance of being incredibly flexible and extraordinarily assertive when negotiating in difficult situations with very challenging people. In the film, Anne Bancroft plays the role of Ann Sullivan who is challenged to communicate with a blind and deaf Helen Keller, masterfully played by Patty Duke. As the story progresses, Helen develops a strong aversion to Ann's teaching methods, much preferring to be with her more indulgent parents. When teaching Helen in her home is clearly not working, Ann removes Helen to a cabin where a contest of wills between the two is played out over a period of two weeks. Even in the new setting, Helen remains unreachable until Ann, demonstrating a great deal of flexibility, continues to change her approach until she finds one that will work. She starts to teach a young black servant named Percy to sign. Helen becomes jealous of Percy thereby establishing Ann as "teacher." Acting does not come any better than that displayed in this film. At the same time, the viewer is exposed to a Master Negotiator dealing with one of the most demanding, intriguing and taxing challenges that any negotiator is likely to face.

The Paper (1994).

The Paper concerns a negotiation for the heart and soul of a newspaper. The main story is about ethics and negotiation style. In this film, Michael Keaton plays a reporter whose main goal is to print accurate news. Glenn Close plays an aggressive assistant editor who is willing to stretch the facts to increase the newspaper's circulation. These characters do an excellent job of playing the roles of the essentially cooperative and aggressive negotiator.

Philadelphia (1993).

Philadelphia is a film about negotiation and advocacy. The story concerns a young lawyer, Andrew Beckett, who is wrongfully dismissed by a prestigious Philadelphia law firm because he has AIDS. The story takes place early in the AIDS epidemic when public understanding of this disease was much less tolerant and sophisticated than it is today. There are several sequences in this movie which illustrate excellent negotiation and communication skills balanced perfectly with well thought out advocacy strategies: for example, the scene where Andrew Beckett's lawyer strongly advocates for the fair treatment of his client while at the same time showing that he understands the defendant's and, by implication, the jury's, misunderstanding and fear of AIDS. A second scene that illustrates these skills is the preparation for the closing arguments. Beckett's brother suggests the analogy of a Top Gun pilot being asked to fly one of the most difficult missions of his or her career as being similar to Andrew Beckett's being asked to take on one of the firm's most difficult cases before he was dismissed. These two scenes illustrate the importance of preparation and the importance of well thought out opening and closing arguments.

Priest (1996).

This is a movie about a young priest who must come to terms with an intense moral dilemma. The priest finds out, through the confessional, that one of the young girls in his parish is being sexually molested by her father. On the one hand, his morals dictate that he tell the authorities. On the other hand, he feels duty-bound to protect the sanctity of the confessional and not disclose what he learned during confession. As the priest tries to resolve this intense moral dilemma, some of the most difficult negotiations he has are with himself. As all negotiators must face ethical and moral issues at some time in their career, this film presents a thorough understanding of just how difficult this process can be, along with some strategies to help resolve these types of complex and difficult issues.

Ransom (1996).

This is a movie about the kidnapping of a child. The father turns the tables on the kidnappers by offering a $2 million ransom for the kidnappers. Although this movie can be difficult to watch for parents and grandparents as it articulates their worst fears, it vividly demonstrates the importance of having a strong BATNA (Best Alternative To a Negotiated Agreement). It also shows the importance of creating options where it seems that only a limited number of options are available.

Schindler's List (1993).

The film presents the incredible but true story of Oskar Schindler, who as a womanizer, war profiteer and member of the Nazi party, saved the lives of more than 1,100 Jews during the Holocaust. During the film, Schindler is transformed into a moral leader who negotiates to save the lives of the Jewish prisoners who work in his factory. Much of Schindler's success rests on his ability to discern the needs and desires of those with whom he negotiates and the artful use of his networking skills to expand his domain of influence.

Searching for Bobby Fischer (1993).

Searching for Bobby Fischer is the story of a child prodigy, his relationships with his parents and his chess teachers, and the discoveries he makes about winning, losing, perseverance, friendship and fear of failure. There are many wonderful scenes in the movie about the negotiation of expectations, the most memorable of which is the organizer of a chess tournament negotiating with the parents regarding what is and is not acceptable parental behaviour. Watching this movie with my 13-year-old son led to a terrific conversation about negotiating our expectations of each other and more importantly negotiating the expectations we place on ourselves.

Stand and Deliver (1988).

This wonderful, heart-warming film is the true story of a dedicated and inspiring teacher who uses his negotiating, advocating, teaching, coaching, mentoring and leadership skills to convince 18 Hispanic students from a poor inner city school to take on the challenge of passing the National Advanced Placement Calculus Exam, even though they function at a remedial level in math.

12 Angry Men (1957).

    12 Angry Men is a classic movie from the 1950s about 12 men on a jury with a seemingly open and shut case. However, one man challenges all of the assumptions and positions of the other jurors and presents them with other options.

Twelve O'Clock High (1949).

    Twelve O'Clock High is the story of how a new commanding officer, Brigadier General Savage, takes over a demoralized bombing unit in World War II. Crucial to the success of his mission, the unit's leader has to lead by example and earn the respect of the men in his unit through the adept use of his leadership, communication and negotiating skills.

TELEVISION SERIES

The West Wing (September 1999 to present).

    The West Wing depicts the decision-making, negotiating, influencing and deal making that goes on behind the scenes in the White House of president Jed Bartlet. The pace is fast and the characters are three-dimensional and real. The program deals with complex issues such as campaign finance reform, the balance between funding for drug treatment versus drug enforcement, and rehabilitation versus mandatory jail sentencing, just to name a few.

---

1 Note that where applicable, information on the most recent edition of a document is contained in square brackets. A more extensive annotated bibliography is available free of charge on the Newsletters Page at www.bradmcrae.com.

Index

About the Author

Dr. Brad McRae holds a doctoral degree in counselling psychology from the Univeristy of British Columbia and was trained in negotiating and influencing at the Harvard Project on Negotiation. He has been teaching *The Seven Strategies of Master Negotiators* for the past 16 years. His teaching has included both the private and public sector and non-profit organizations. He also taught all levels of government: municipal, provincial and federal. Brad has taught negotiating skills worldwide, including in Canada, the United States, Mexico and Africa.

Delivering over 100 days of staff training and keynote addresses per year, Brad has some very prestigious clients. He developed a course specifically for the Canadian National Railroad and has delivered courses in negotiating, influencing and facilitating skills for the McGill University Health Centre. Brad also conducts all the staff training in negotiating and influencing skills for Michelin North America in Canada and the United States. His other client groups include accounting, banking and financial, communication, education, governments, healthcare, manufacturing, pharmaceuticals, retail, social services and volunteer organizations.

Brad's previous titles include *How to Write a Thesis and Keep Your Sanity* and *Practical Time Management*, which sold in Canada, the United States, Hong Kong, India and Poland. *Negotiating and Influencing Skills* was published in the United States. Brad is also the editor and publisher of *The Negotiation Newsletter*.

Brad currently teaches at St. Mary's University at the World Trade Centre and is a subject matter expert in negotiating and influencing skills at the Pearson International Peacekeeping Centre. He is also a member of the Canadian Association of Professional Speakers and the International Association of Professional Speakers. Brad is president of McRae & Associates Inc., a firm specializing in keynotes and staff training and development in the United States and Canada.

Brad lives in Halifax, Nova Scotia, with his son and daughter.

For information about Keynotes and Seminars on "The Seven Strategies of Master Negotiators," "High Impact Presentation Skills," or "Optimum EQ: Developing and Enhancing Your Emotional Intelligence," contact Brad McRae by phone at (902) 423-4680 or by fax at (902) 484-7915. Our mailing address is: 5880 Spring Garden Road, Suite 400, Halifax, Nova Scotia, Canada, B3H 1Y1. Or you can e-mail at **brad@bradmcrae.com**, or visit our website **www.bradmcrae.com**.